So, We Only Have a Few Minutes Left

~~John H. Stuhl, Ph.D.~~

~~Dr. John H. Stuhl~~

Dr. John ❓

Dr. J ✓

John ✗

Middy May Publishing
11318 Ford's Cove Lane
Farragut, TN 37934

Library of Congress Cataloging-inPublication
Data available.

Printed in the United States of America

For You

So, We Only Have a Few Minutes Left
John H. Stuhl, Ph.D.

For over twenty-six years, it has been my honor and privilege to practice as a psychologist and therapist. For me, the work has been the most meaningful and fulfilling endeavor of my life, other than being a husband and father, and now grandfather! I have loved getting up in the mornings to go to work, I have looked forward to seeing you, my patients, I have found myself happily working through solutions and strategies to assist you in your changes and healing.

I haven't always been successful...I know you are more aware of that than I am. I haven't always been who you've needed, or wanted me to be. I'm certain that all too often, I was unintentionally frustrating, or maddening, or annoying. All too often, I was dense or imperceptive, or stubborn or slow to hear you out. For those times, I do apologize. Hopefully, though, you did experience that I never stopped caring about you and your needs, that I never gave up on you, I always hoped that what we did together would help you to heal and find happiness, even if sometimes my efforts didn't match my desire.

No, I haven't always been successful, and I do hate that, because I hate, hated, not bringing about the healing and changes that you needed and wanted. And still, hopefully, my work has made a difference for you.

I have never stopped being amazed that people would seek me out and ask for help, that you would share with me your most horrific experiences and damaging times and your most painful wounds. I have always felt gratitude that I have gotten to do this work, and felt so appreciative of you, that you would let me work with you, and that you would return each week to continue your healing. Each time that happened, each time you asked to reschedule, to come back, to continue therapy, I felt humbled. I don't know if I showed that, but it's true. My work, and your trust, belief, and faith in me, was so humbling to me. It still is, and always will be. And it is such an honor.

And now, I'm retiring, and it has been a very difficult decision. I have loved this life as a psychologist, as your therapist. Absolutely loved it. And I'm going to miss it. I'm going to miss you. For the longest time, I put off the decision to retire, because my work has been so fulfilling. But, as I've shared with most of you, I have a third career I yearn for, and it is time to move on to that. As much as I've loved being your therapist and psychologist, I love writing and creating stories also.

Unfortunately, I can't do both. There are some people who can balance two loves in their lives, both their vocation and their avocation. And while I wish I was one of them, I have accepted that I'm not. I can't remain a practicing psychologist, and do the writing (and book pimping) that is necessary to be successful because for so long, being a therapist has been my first love. If I continue as a therapist, deciding *I'll simply cut back to three days a week* I will fail in that commitment. As long as I'm practicing psychology, if someone calls and needs help, I'm going to expand my hours to help them. To begin my third career, I have to end my second.

But how do I say goodbye? How do I let go? How do I tell you thank you, and how much I've appreciated you, how much you've meant to me? And then I had a brainstorm. Well, probably more like a brain fart. I thought, *You know, I could jot down some of the guiding principles and skills that I've used in my work, share the truths that I believe, and include some of the bullshit I've made up. And then, give each person, give you, a copy.*

It may be worthless. It may suck so bad you won't want to ruin a good fire by burning it. That's okay; I can't control your choices of what to do with it. If I write this well enough, I'll feel fulfilled that I've given the best gift I can, even if the gift is kind of myopic on insight and thin on knowledge and wisdom. I'll feel I've given you one last "the best that I can," and I'll hope it is helpful to you, and useful to you. And that you'll feel the love and passion and belief, the respect and care and appreciation I've felt for you all these years.

It's my one last gift of therapy, of psychology. And, it's a beautiful bridge, at least for me, to move from therapist to writer.

So, here goes…a few meanderings of my mind. I suspect a lot of this will be familiar to you. That's okay, because it means I've been consistent over the years. Some of these ideas and concepts may be new to you, which may mean in our sessions together they didn't come up, or possibly that I botched my work with you, you got shorted, and now you might feel screwed. If this is the case, then, my apologies.

Most importantly, what I share here is what I believe. These beliefs are what I find true, what I experience as most important and influential. It does not mean that what is true for me is true for you. In sharing these thoughts, I hope that you hear the same thing you heard in therapy, that I share these concepts not to tell you "how you should believe" or "how you should change" (we'll get to "should's" in a bit), but what I've found to be true for me. The most important concept, at least for me, is that you find what is true for you. I hope you use these ideas as a means to discover your own truth, whether your truth is similar to mine, or markedly distinct from mine.

Thank you, for this life's work and being able to share it with you. Thank you, for your trust and belief in me. And thank you, for inviting me into your life and allowing me to be a part of it, albeit how small. It may sound cliché, but I truly know I've learned as much from you as you from me, and I am grateful for all I've learned and experienced and been able to share.

Thank you.

The Classic Disclaimer

There are multiple examples in the next few pages. Examples that I draw from my years of working with patients. It is absolutely essential for me to state: if you think one example is "you," YOU ARE MISTAKEN!

I say this not just for the liability protection I've been told I need, but also because it is true. All the examples I give of patient interactions and experiences are such a mishmash of people, such a conglomerate of experiences, that none of them are representative of a single patient.

The same is true for names. I know, a few of you have asked me, "Dr. J, you're gonna give me my own chapter, aren't you? I mean, I've given you enough material for at least a *chapter*. Oh, and I'd like my name on it." Well, uh, no, I can't do that. I think that's called unethical or something. Therefore, all the names used herein are made up as well. So, if you find yourself resonating with an example, and think "Oh, my God, that's me Dr. J's talking about!", I suggest it is simply that the examples identify some universal struggles and challenges that all humans face. As such, I'm glad you resonate with them, because it means I'm on track with what I'm presenting, and it could possibly, maybe, kinda be of help to you.

A Warning!

This book is full of prayer language.

Prayer language?

Yes, prayer language. If you've never heard me say this in a session, then I have failed you as a therapist and a human. I tell (or try to tell) all my patients that in therapy, there is no profanity (other than some unexpectedly profane words, which you'll hear about soon). In therapy... of course, I believe all of life is therapy, so I practice this discipline every waking moment... in therapy, to curse, to cuss, is to use prayer language.

My editor, mentor, friend, muse and master-of-my-imaginings asked me to explain why profanity is "prayer language." Even though none of *you* ever needed an explanation, I have a compulsion to comply and meet other's needs. Thus, I offer this explanation. Prayer is in its most fundamental sense, chatting up god. Not just talking to god, or the deity, or the universe, or Captain Kirk (however you want to imagine it), it is listening also. It is sharing, and receiving. It is hearing, and learning, and knowing. And prayer, if it's truly authentic, brings powerful relief and wisdom. It brings freedom. It brings liberation (yes, those are slightly different). It brings joy and understanding and

11

fulfillment. Which is exactly what the healthy use of profanity does for us. To pray, using the prayer language I encourage, is to find both an outlet that relieves, and a liberation that transforms.

This book is full of prayer language. I deliberated for a long, long time (approximately twelve minutes) whether to write this as I would and *have* said it to you, all these years. You've been in therapy with me, after all; you know that I pray, and in biblical terms, I pray without ceasing.

So, as you begin to plod through this tome, *if* you choose to wade through this morass of words, be aware. Be warned: there is praying within. I hope the prayers bring you the same liberation, the same relief and release that prayers bring me. And I hope your own praying will become unceasing.

And now, on to the word jumble.

On Feelings

Of course a therapist is going to start with feelings!

But why? Why are feelings so important? Why do I (and many other therapists) harp on them?

For me, the reason to begin with feelings is that they are such powerful influences in our lives, and possibly the most misunderstood. They move us, they drive us, they compel us, and they often operate without our awareness, outside of our conscious mind.

But that doesn't mean we are just stuck with them, or have no control over them, no choices about them. It does not mean we are powerless in relation to our feelings; after all, if that were the case, we'd be little better than all the other animals on the planet, subject to instincts and urges that we don't make conscious decisions about.

Maybe the best place to begin is to identify what I believe about feelings. As I'll say repeatedly in the next few (or many) pages, when I share my beliefs, it doesn't mean that you have to agree with those beliefs. I mean, what do I know: I'm only a Counseling Psychologist with two Masters degrees, one Ph.D., and 26 years of experience (I hope you hear that joke and irony in my voice).

Here are my beliefs about feelings, the reasons for these, and some explanations of how this information can be useful in healing and growth.

I use the term "feeling" as mostly synonymous with "emotions" and "drives." All these wonderful powers within us arise out of the same place, our primitive or lizard or primal brain. So, when we feel a "drive," an "urge," when we are "compelled" and feel a "compulsion," we are experiencing a primal feeling that developed over eons of evolution. These drives are survival mechanisms in their raw form: anger/rage to help defend ourself against attacks, anxiety/fear to help us be alert for dangers to our life, attraction/lust to reproduce and help extend the existence of the species.

But that was eons ago. Over the years, we humans have evolved to develop a modern brain (at least that's the theory). This evolved brain is where we make executive decisions, where we moderate emotions and feelings and drives, and this modern brain allows us to create and maintain societies.

All this is to establish a simple basis of understanding, of the origin of feelings and emotions. Here are some of my beliefs that arise out of this basic understanding.

First, feelings are amoral. They are neither right or wrong, neither good or bad. They simply emerge in our life. Our challenge is to listen to our feelings and choose what to do with them, and how to act on them. More on this in a moment.

Second, feelings are not facts. I may have a feeling, and it be inaccurate. Let's use an example: a woman suffers a rape, and as she is healing from this evil, she discovers she feels ashamed (I believe every person who has suffered a sexual assault has felt this at one time or another). The feeling is real; however, *it is not accurate!* A person who has suffered an assault is a victim, and a victim is always innocent. It is understandable that a person who has been molested feels ashamed. That feeling emerges because there is often the lingering thought that they should have prevented the assault, they should have stopped it. That negative belief is also inaccurate. Most often, what lies behind the belief that the victim should have prevented the assault is the desire, and wish, that *if* they could have stopped it, prevented it, they would have. Of course that's true. But that is not what happened. It is hard for us to accept that we have been the victim of an assault.

Let's return to the feeling of shame a person feels when having been molested. The feeling is real, but inaccurate, because the underlying negative belief is inaccurate. As the person changes that belief, from self-blame to self-acceptance, the feelings of shame and embarrassment and guilt dissipate. They are resolved, and the person is no longer burdened by those feelings.

My third belief about feelings: we don't choose what we feel. Our feelings emerge from within our psyche; they arise within us without conscious thought, choice or decision. This is another reason why feelings are amoral. It is also the reason why it is so essential for us to accept our feelings just as they are, and not judge them. If they simply emerge from within us, we aren't choosing what we feel. However, this does not mean we are powerless in relation to our feelings. We are not. We can choose how to act on our feelings. We can choose to moderate our feelings. We can learn how to identify and acknowledge a feeling, we learn how to investigate and question a feeling, and most importantly, we learn how to resolve and dismiss feelings. And, we can learn how to build healthy cognitive structures that allow the feelings that emerge within us to be more and more aligned with health.

My fourth belief. There are no "bad" feelings. There are no "negative" feelings. Every feeling we have serves a positive purpose, even those feelings that are uncomfortable or that hurt or torture us. To choose this belief allows us to embrace our feelings, whatever they are, and not to flee from them or hide from them or be fearful of them. For when we embrace a feeling, we actually reduce the intensity just a bit, possibly just a single iota. Which means we are not powerless in relation to that intense feeling.

What's an iota? I've actually had more than one of you ask me that. One patient put it quite succinctly: "What the fuck is an iota?!" The classic definition is that an iota is an infinitesimal amount. Or, a really small unit. When my patient asked me, I said, "Hey, I'll show you what an iota is. Take a breath." He thought I was trying to calm him down; I wasn't really. (Though, as you know, an intentional breath can reduce anxiety. Maybe by one iota, but that's an effect). My patient took a breath. I could see the tension in his body release, just a small amount. And then I said, "That breath? That's an iota. Every time you take a breath, you defeat anxiety's effort to kill you, because that's the way we tend to experience anxiety (especially when our anxiety is elevated), that anxiety is out to kill us. So, in human terms (for me, at least), an iota is a single breath. And, every breath we take is an affirmation of life.

Fifth belief: we always have at least one feeling occurring at any moment, and often more than one. The challenge of life, and healing, is to identify our feelings and accept them. This is difficult, because there are feelings that scare us in their intensity, or because of what we think they mean about us. (My word queen, aka editor, declared that last phrase is of extreme importance. So I thought I'd identify that). However, identifying a feeling, admitting a feeling exists in us that we are uncomfortable with, gives us power in relation to our feelings.

Sixth belief: feelings do not have to make sense. They don't have to be logical or line up rationally or realistically. As humans, we have a fundamental need to organize our beliefs in reasonable, rational structures (though we often don't act like we have). We like order and consistency in our belief structures. But our feelings aren't like that. We can have two absolutely contradictory feelings at the same time. For example, we can have feelings of disapproval and dislike for someone, and also have feelings of very strong sexual attraction to that person. Just as confounding, as my goddess of words points out, we can even have compound feelings— bittersweet, angrily surprised, fearfully disgusted, rap music.

This can be confusing! That is why it is especially helpful to accept that our feelings don't have to make sense, or be reasonable, or rational. When we accept this concept, we free ourselves to identify, accept and embrace our feelings just as they are. Which, as I've said before, gives us much more freedom and power to choose what to do with them. And, it can help to clarify matters for us, because my definition of confusion with regards to humans and our psyches is: confusion is when there are two or more feelings, or beliefs, or both, wound up together like a braided rope. The way to bring understanding out of confusion is to separate out those feelings and thoughts, so they can be seen individually. When we do this, we get clarity and our choices of what we will do open up.

Those are my fundamental thoughts about feelings. Hope this makes sense, and is helpful. Now, on to cognitions.

Beliefs

Beliefs are cognitions.

But not all cognitions are beliefs.

We have thousands of beliefs. Thousands and thousands. Most of them, we don't have to attend to, because the aspect of life to which they pertain is so consistent and stable that the belief becomes a part of the ground of our existence. Here's an example: the belief that $2 + 2 = 4$. We learned that in first grade; well, for me, probably fourth grade. It doesn't change and aside from an exceptionally few theoretical mathematicians, we don't ever question this belief. We just act on it, rely on it.

There are neurological scientists who say that there are hundreds of thousands, even into the millions, of cognitions occurring in our brains every second. Scientists also estimate that approximately twenty-five hundred of these cognitions are available to our conscious mind at any moment. There are cognitions in our subconscious, and some in our unconscious mind, that we at times can bring to our awareness, but most of the time we're operating on the twenty-five hundred. And some of the cognitions we don't need or even want to be aware of. We don't need to monitor every heartbeat, or when to raise or lower our blood pressure.

So much is managed by our brain and the cognitions that maintain our physical existence. That's excellent, and amazing. As one person put it, our brain is an organ that secretes thoughts. I like that. The challenge is what do we do with those secretions.

The cognitions we most struggle with are the beliefs, most of which are chosen, either unknowingly via upbringing and history and culture and experience, and some that we intentionally choose. It is this set of beliefs that can help us heal, or stymie our growth and progress.

Let's begin with my beliefs about beliefs. (I know. I know. I'm using the word "beliefs" a lot! My editor has told me so. I am struggling to find synonyms that are appropriate and helpful, without destroying the flow of information. I'm not sure I'm being successful, but I'll keep trying. I invite you to simply work with me, tolerate my overuse of "beliefs," and accept that I'm doing the best I can to make this read as smoothly as possible. Which, believe me, I am trying to accomplish).

First, I believe that we as humans have an innate need to make order out of things. We don't like chaos, at least most of us don't, and we seek order. There are many studies that indicate how humans are innately inclined to complete incomplete figures, and impose an order out of something that was actually random.

This need to create order and structure extends to our beliefs. We have a drive or need to structure our thoughts in a cogent and coherent manner. We have a need to order our beliefs, for them to be systematic and consistent and logical. However, I also believe that we aren't the best at sustaining our belief structures and adapting them as we grow and learn and change.

My second belief about beliefs: many beliefs we hold are biased and inaccurate, but we've never really actively assessed them, and so they lie beneath our awareness, influencing our perceptions of the world and our feelings. They have a significant effect on us. Part of the process of therapy, as I'm sure you're aware from our work together, is bringing to awareness the beliefs we carry, examining them and deciding if they are healthy or unhealthy, if they help us or harm us, if they lead to healing or prevent healing.

Third belief about beliefs. There are beliefs that are healthier than others. And there are some beliefs that are simply flat out inaccurate, especially beliefs we hold about ourselves. For example, we hold many negative beliefs about ourselves in our subconscious and unconscious minds. We have subsumed, or absorbed, these beliefs from our culture, from messages we have received from adults when we were children, from religions. We've ingested them, and they've become inculcated within us. Okay, that was too fancy. We've swallowed them whole and the negative self-beliefs have become lodged in our minds. In psychology, we call this: Not Good.

A fourth belief about beliefs is related to the third. Negative beliefs about ourselves help to sustain painful emotions, especially the most painful of the emotions, guilt, embarrassment and shame. To resolve and dismiss these emotions, we must find the negative self-beliefs and change them.

Fifth belief: we can choose what we believe, unlike feelings, which we don't choose. Feelings emerge within us, out of our basic drives and urges and belief sets we have adopted.

Prove it, you say? Okay. Did you choose with whom you fell in love? Do you choose whom you find attractive? Was it your mind or your emotions that led you to feel attraction and fall in love? Yes, it can be both. But that's not the point, smartass. It's a rhetorical question. The answer is: it was your feelings.

The importance of this is that when we choose healthy beliefs, our emotions are likewise healthier, more balanced, and the painful ones can be resolved. When we choose healthy self-beliefs, we have more accurate and true feelings about ourself. We are less critical and judgmental (the goal, of course, is to eliminate all judgement and criticism); we are more accepting of ourself. And the more we are accepting of ourselves, the more we can be accepting of others.

Behaviors

Well, this should be easier. And it is. Mostly.

Behaviors are what we *do*. They are the ways we in *act* in the world. However, there are other activities that I believe are behaviors. Unsurprisingly, these are combinations of feelings and cognitions.

I tell parents, when working to help them develop and improve parenting skills, that a child's attitude is a behavior also. Why, you ask? Great question. The reason is that as we are raising our children, we are helping them to develop healthy attitudes and perspectives. We don't want to control what they think; however, we do want to direct and shape their views. And those views/attitudes/beliefs about themselves shape their behaviors towards other people.

Children who believe that they should get whatever they want have attitudes of specialness and entitlement. Such a child will likely behave towards others with indifference, insensitivity, inattentiveness, and condescension. The child is special; others are there to serve him or her.

When working with our children, it is vital to identify their unhealthy attitudes in simple ways, because the younger a child is, the less she or he can understand cognitively the intricacies and complexity of attitudes and behaviors.

Children can, though, understand that the way they are acting (in their attitude) is unacceptable, and they can change their attitude, their way of being and communicating.

Of course, the older one gets, the more this simple concept becomes complex and intricate. We can have an attitude of superiority or entitlement that communicates to others that they are inferior, that they are not as important as us. We may not *act* in such a way (cutting in line in front of people, taking something we want out of another's hand, making it obvious we are ignoring someone intentionally) and yet still communicate emotionally that we feel superior or better than another. This could be called *emotional behaviors*, I guess. Or, maybe it's better to identify that emotional *expressions* are behaviors. If we wanted to get very specific, we could break down the *behaviors* that we choose (in our tone of voice, the way we look at someone, the physical stance we take in relation to another, etc.) to express our emotions.

But I don't want to get that specific, because it is too easy for me to get caught up in the weeds trying to explain all of it. And, truthfully, I'm probably not smart enough to develop all the specific and detailed steps and strategies to do the task justice. I'll just leave the description of behaviors as those things we *do*, both the actions we take physically and the way we express ourselves emotionally.

Stuhlisms

For nearly three decades, I've developed beliefs that guide me. I've created these "Stuhlisms from both my study of psychology, my attending to the wisdom of others (especially you, my patients), and out of my own experiences…which is a fancy way of saying what I've told all of you at one time or another: I make shit up.

These little aphorisms are all mine. They are truths to me (except for those exceptions that I myself deem appropriate). Once more, my editor guru and the one to whom I bend the knee, has said she "doesn't understand what I mean" by my joke above. So let me explain. As I have said earlier (or maybe it's later), there are no absolutes; there are always exceptions to a rule. By my playfully stating that the truths I offer are truths, except where they are not, I am actually communicating that we all make exceptions in our beliefs. It is essential that we recognize when we make exceptions, why we make those exceptions, and if our exceptions are ones we need or want to keep, if they are helpful to us and our relationships, or harmful to them. So, these truths I offer to you are not absolutes, but possible guidelines for your own healing, choosing, and living.

Also important to note: you may have heard these or some form of these in our therapy, and now, upon reading them, think, "I believe Dr. John had a different number on that Stuhlism." That may be true. Because, as I just said, I make shit up, and my creation one day may have been differently numbered than another day. In fact, the *real* truth is that I make up the numbers as I go along, so you can basically ignore them. They don't really indicate any hierarchy of "truth'"; the numbers are just part of the fun. However, I realize that such fun in real life does not translate well into a written document. Therefore, the numbers here are in sequential order, to simplify matters and keep you from a migraine.

As I share these, know that I may have also left out one Stuhlism you heard me share/create in a session. That's because, 1. I make this shit up as I go along; 2. I make this shit up in the moment, to address the specific need that is occurring in therapy at that moment; and 3. I have never written these aphorisms down before. This is my first attempt at recording them. If I've left one out you heard, and think it is either very important and helpful, or especially misguided, call and tell me. If it's just one that had little significance...well, then, you have better things to do with your time. It probably wasn't worth remembering anyway—

which begs the question: What are you doing remembering stupid shit I said?! You might want to get some therapy for that.

Stuhlisms…and here we go.

Stuhlism #1

People are …

In therapy, I usually follow this with…"stupid." That's because in therapy I am aligning with a patient's struggles, in order to help healing. People need to feel heard. That's one hundred and seventeen times truer in therapy. So, I align so that patients recognize I hear, feel, and understand their pain.

If you were with me for a longer period of time, you probably heard me expand this first Stuhlism. To do it justice, here is what it really is.

Stuhlism #1

People are…

stupid
amazing
a mess
a blessing
maddening
a gift
confusing as hell
wonderful
surprising in the most beautiful of ways

The list could go on and on. There are an unending number of adjectives we could use to describe humans, and almost every one of them would be accurate. So, to use a single one would be incomplete. One aspect of healing is to identify what are our present beliefs, and make adjustments when appropriate. A huge adjustment is to recognize that whenever we lump all people together, we are doing them and ourselves an injustice. Almost every person has more complexity and aspects of self than can be captured in a single descriptor.

In fact, this belief leads to another.

Stuhlism #57 (Remember, the numbers are without purpose, except to possibly provide a tag for our mind. And I placed this one here, out of order, just to remind you. Isn't that fun?) **There are no absolutes. Possibly including this one**.

The goal of this aphorism to help us catch ourselves from making global and comprehensive statements, such as:

You never say anything nice about me.

You always say no to sex.

Everyone is against me.

All of them hate me.

No one cares.

These statements are harmful, because if we are working through a conflict with someone, or working through some hurt or emotional wound, such a statement of an absolute allows no room for change, no possibility of a different perspective. And, thus, we remain stuck. Which, in the words of one of my patients, is "not fun."

Stuhlism #3

If we want to find healing, we track pain.

This one is difficult. Who wants to track pain? Who wants to go to those places in their memories, in their lives, in their hearts, where they hurt the most?

No one, really. Actually, to exercise Stuhlism #57 above, few of us do. Our normal response is to avoid pain, to escape hurt. That's why we have defense mechanisms, to protect us.

Paradoxically, hurt and emotional pain serve us by guiding us to where we need to heal. In life, we suffer emotional wounds. There is no escaping this reality. Some of the hurts we suffer are healed by our unconscious processes. For example, as a child, we are snapped at by our parent and we cry because "our feelings have been hurt." Then, if we had good parents, we are later comforted and soothed, and that hurt is resolved.

There are other times in life where the hurt is so severe that it overwhelms our natural healing mechanisms. These are times when trauma occurs, or when there is such confusion and anguish that our natural healing systems of the mind (the Adaptive Information Processing Capacity) either stall or are made ineffective. For elucidation, Adaptive Information Processing is our mind's capacity to take an experience, gather the cognitive information we need from that experience, and then literally metabolize, or wash out that which we don't need, which are the feelings and physical sensations we experienced in that event. Let me give an example.

I'm five again, and about to learn how to ride a bicycle. My father is there, encouraging me (that's a part of the experience and every aspect of an experience is a neural network in our mind), I'm feeling very anxious (neural network), my brother is chanting "spaz, spaz, spaz" (another neural network). I get on the bike, go to ride, and lose my balance (another neural network). I fall (another neural network). I scrape my knee (neural network). I see the blood (neural network). I feel pain (neural network). I bang my head (neural network) and it throbs (neural network).

My dad helps me up and says "Okay, John, let's try again." I look at the bicycle and my head throbs more (nothing touched my head; it's just that the neural network in my mind is activated by the thought of trying to ride again). My pain in my knee increases (activation of that neural network). I start again, I catch my balance, I ride and I feel exuberance.

My mind (thank you, evolution and all other contributing factors) takes the first experience of my falling off the bicycle, extracts the one bit of information it needs, and literally metabolizes/washes out all the other aspects of the experience. The bit of information my mind keeps? That falling off the bicycle hurts. My mind dismisses the sensation of pain of the first experience, the anxiety, and the negative messages from my wonderful brother. I don't need to keep those; all I need is the *information, the knowledge* that falling off the bicycle hurts.

That's how Adaptive Information Processing works. That is what Adaptive Information Processing is in practice.

And yes, I can ride a bicycle now without anxiety.

The wounds I mentioned before the example are the wounds we deal with the most in therapy. And, in therapy, with these emotional hurts and wounds, we track the pain we feel.

Why? What benefit is it to track pain?

Well, to heal a wound, we have to find its source, and identify its scope. Pain will take us back to the experience, to the occasion, where the wound occurred. Once there, we can begin to look at what that experience meant to us. We can look at what beliefs sustain the hurt. We can decide what meaning we will make of it, what beliefs we will create and choose to decrease the pain. We can identify specific steps in how to heal the emotional pain, be it hurt or anger, shame or guilt, anxiety or anguish.

All this occurs when we identify our pain, follow it to its source and take action to make changes there.

Stuhlism #4

Life is not fair. ("Wait! Everyone and their dead cousin knows life is not fair. There's no wisdom there, Dr. J." And I say, "You are correct! But let me finish.") **Life is not fair. Life is not unfair either. Life just is.**

Life just is, filled with unfairness, injustices, wrongs, evil, and also filled with undeserved advantages, unearned benefits, freely gifted blessings and wonder and worth beyond reason.

Do I need to explain this further? It is a crucial principle that I believe provides a great deal of balance and liberation in life. It helps us to moderate lows and losses, and temper highs and successes.

I'm now officially tired of generating Stuhlisms. Oh, there are more (and I'll add this last one), but let me weave them into the next chapters and see if I can't make them a bit more applicable as I go along. But before I go, I offer you...

Stuhlism #5

We cannot change another person. ("Once again, John, you've stated what everyone and all those dead cousins know." Sooo, the second part of this Stuhlism is the crucial element). **However, if we attend to what we say, and what we do, and are very intentional about it, we can evoke an enormous amount of change in others and evoke in our lives a great deal of what we want and desire.**

Now, that sounds significant, huh?! And enticing. The crucial aspect of this Stuhlism is that we *pay attention to ourselves and the changes **we** make!*

It is so easy for us to get focused externally, to focus on others, on what we want *him* to change, and how we want *her* to be different. Our attention becomes captured by and our efforts become dominated by the changes *we want to see in others*. However, since we and all the dead know we can't change another, when we focus our attention and efforts there, on external changes, in the words of one semi-intelligent genius (yeah, that'd be me), "We're screwed."

The task, the challenge, is to keep our focus on ourself, on how we can change, on what we can do differently. Then, if we pay attention to our changes, *and the consequent differences in others in response to how we think and act differently,* we can determine what changes of ours bring about desired results.

Some might say, "Hey, that's just manipulation." Okay, but is manipulation always a negative thing?! It is certainly most often considered a negative activity. But, really, it doesn't have to be. Manipulation doesn't have to be deceptive, or solely self-benefiting or self-centered.

Let's look at an example, and then move on to some other ideas. Let's say that I've gotten into a habit of arguing with my best friend, which I find unpleasant and off-putting, and that she finds aggravating. Initially, I do what all of us do, and I think about how difficult my friend is being, and how if she would just stop being so confrontive, or stop being so defensive, then the arguments would stop. If she would just stop being so negative, or being so sensitive; if she would just stop being (fill in the blank), and start being (fill in the blank), then everything would be fine.

However, I can't make my best friend change in the ways I want. I can't *make* my best friend (fill in the blank/do a damn thing). I can't force her to listen, or hear, or understand me, or make any other cognitive or behavioral change I want. I can't do that, because no matter what I try, I can't change my best friend.

And yet, *I can change me!* If we're frequently arguing, I can look at why *I* argue, I can look at what *I'm* doing and thinking before and during an argument, and I can decide to shift what I am doing, and do something different. If I realize I start to raise my voice when my friend raises her voice, I can change and intentionally make my voice become softer when she raises her voice. If I realize I stand up and start pointing at her when discussions begin, I can make myself sit down. I can sit on my hands. I can cut off my fingers so I won't point (I'm not recommending this—it seems an extreme change).

As I change what I do, how I think, and how I feel, I pay attention to the effect of my changes on my best friend. If sitting down evokes a quieter tone from my friend, then we are now discussing instead of arguing, and therefore we are listening more rather than explaining more, and trying to understand more rather than trying to be understood.

The result is that my interactions with my best friend become pleasant again, a result that I believe she also appreciates and enjoys. So, my changes evoke changes, and the more I make my choices intentional and healthy, the more I evoke health and enjoyment in my relationships.

Now, the reality is that my best friend may enjoy the arguing, and dislike more pleasant, peaceful, and fun interactions. In that case, I can simply say: she won't be my best friend anymore. If my healthy changes aren't reciprocated, then I need to go where health is more valued and treasured. Which may mean a big change in me: changing best friends.

And now, on to some other aspects of living, healing, and thriving.

Language Matters

What we say, how we say it, the words we choose, the tone and cadence we use all shape the effectiveness of our communications.

"Well, duh, John!"

While shifts in language are quite simple, they are not nearly as easy as we would like. This is one of the reasons I pay such particular attention to the language used in counseling. I'm not referring to profanity; as all of you know, I actually support the use of profanity. As I've told you (probably seventeen times, so I don't need to remind you of this), in therapy, profanity is prayer language. Of course, I think it is prayer language *all* the time, not just during sessions, but that's for another chapter. In therapy, I support and even encourage the use of profanity, because it often gives the needed expressive release that we seek and need.

I had one patient who was in a very public profession, where she had to be highly professional, cautious, and very selective in the language she chose. As she became comfortable accepting my encouragements to pray in therapy, she opened up so much more to her truer, deeper feelings. And she found that healing in and of itself.

One session, she sat down, clearly agitated and steaming. Before I could even ask about it, she launched into these comments about the higher ups at her place of employment: "These stupid fucking morons have NO CLUE what they're doing! They are such dumb shits! Shit, it just pisses me the fuck off!"

She continued for an impressive amount of time. Finally spent, she flopped back into the chair, looked me in the eyes and with a deep sigh and a cleansing breath, said, "Oh, God—it feels *so good* to cuss!" We both spent the next several minutes laughing. The rest of the session was some of the best therapeutic work she had done all year.

The point, you ask? Well, the point is, language is powerful, and when we attend to what we say and how we say it, we increase our power to create our lives the way we want them to be.

Here are some of the skills I believe and have taught with regards to language.

The Skill of "I" Language

When we interact with others, and when we are working through our conflicts with others, we tend to fill our language with "he," "she," "they," "them," "their," "all of them," "others," and "you"(around here, it's more commonly "y'all").

What's wrong with this? What's wrong with using these pronouns? It's not wrong, per se (because I strive to stay away from right and wrong). It is just, most of the time, not helpful. In fact, the use of these pronouns can actually intensify arguments and conflicts.

Let me give an example. I'm in a disagreement with a friend, Sam, and say to him, "You know, you really hurt my feelings." There are two difficulties with this statement: first, I used "you," and secondly, I made my friend responsible for my emotion (which I'll get to next).   When I say "you hurt my feelings" I'm telling my friend what he did, whether that was what he intended or not. In fact, I'm pretty certain none of my good friends would intentionally try to hurt me. If they do, well then, hell, I wanna know about it. And take them off my "good friend" list.

What I've wanted to communicate to my friend is that I am struggling with the emotion of hurt, be it rejection or criticism or embarrassment. Using the skill of "I Language," I can much more effectively share this. "You know, Sam (who is my good friend), I really felt hurt when you said I was only your medium friend, not a good friend."

By stating my feeling this way, I remove blame from Sam, and I take ownership of my feeling. Instead of accusing, I am sharing. I am disclosing something about myself to Sam, which is often much more effective than declaring what he has done to me, whether in his mind he had or hadn't.

To catch ourselves when we speak is a challenge; when we accept that challenge and shift our language, we can affect our relationships powerfully and positively. Let's see if I can give some examples where I restructure the sentence into "I Language":

> You ought to know me by now!
> I Language: I feel very misunderstood.

> Don't you even care what I'm feeling?
> I Language: I am pretty hurt, and I'm feeling rejected.

> Y'all are all out to get me.
> I Language: I'm feeling persecuted. And criticized.

> No one cares.
> I Language: I feel all alone, and not cared about.

> You can't tell me what I think!
> I Language: I have a different opinion.

I could go on, but that would be annoying. Hopefully, you're remembering this from our times together. The crux of this skill is to speak for myself, using "I Language". Try it; it's fun.

The Skill of Positive Statements

What I've encouraged over the years is that we learn to hear our own talk, our own statements, so that we can shift what we say and make our communication more powerful. So many times in life, we express ourselves via negative statements. I'm asked, "What do you want for dinner?" If I respond with, "Well, I don't want Norwegian food tonight," I've told my dinner companion something specific, but not very helpful. First, what the hell is Norwegian food—salted fish? Braised reindeer? Something baked with snow? Second, I have told my (now retreating) dinner companion what I *don't* want. But not what I *do* want. The first, what I don't want, rules out one option (probably also because it's hard to find a really good Norwegian restaurant around here), but it leaves thousands of options open and the question unresolved. Think how much more significant it is to convert the sentence, freeing it of negatives, so that it is more powerful and helpful. "Well, I still don't want Norwegian food tonight, but <here comes the conversion> I would like Asian fusion food." Now my dinner companion (if they've come back) has a very clear idea of what I'd like.

Why do we so often talk in negatives, saying what we don't want, what we don't like, what we don't believe and not sharing what we do want, like, believe? I think we do this for several reasons. We think we're being nice, courteous, because if we say what we want then somehow that makes a demand of the other person (btw, we ended up with street tacos that night). This idea is noble, yet incorrect. Simply sharing what we want does not make a demand of another; it actually helps the other person to understand more clearly.

A second reason we often talk in negatives is we're not sure what we want. We don't stop to listen to ourselves (Oh, listening to ourselves is sooo important! That's one I'll yammer on about later.), and so we give an automatic response. Or, we offer an ambiguous response so we don't have to listen to ourselves, because listening to ourselves is hard work. And sometimes scary.

A third reason we may speak in negatives is to protect ourselves. When we say what we want, we can feel a bit vulnerable. What if the other person thinks what we want is dumb, or mean, or wrong? We are afraid of getting judged or criticized, and so rather than experience that, we hide what we want or think.

Of course, this is counterproductive. If we are trying improve our communications and make life and relationships heathier and happier, we want to learn how to be more open, more transparent, not less. Hopefully, I'll say more about vulnerability and openness later—if I don't forget. However, you do realize I'm getting on in years and may have that thing?... what is it called?...something about memory?....where you can't?....Oh, never mind. I can't remember.

An example! I had a patient who was sharing with me her difficulties with intimacy. But instead, let's say it was food. I think it will be easier to present this as food, because that way we'll eliminate the possible complications of differing beliefs about what are healthy and appropriate sexual beliefs and behaviors. As I was saying, this patient shared with me her difficulties with food. As I gathered history, she was telling me about a person with whom she'd had an occasion to eat cake. I asked, "Well, when you went over to his room, you thought you were just going to hang out. You didn't think there'd be cake. But, did you want to eat cake?"

Her answer was, "Well, I wouldn't have eaten cake if I hadn't wanted to." Not just a negative sentence. A *double* negative sentence!

So I asked, "Are you saying that you wanted to have cake?" She said, "Yes. Isn't that what I said?"

And I explained to her the differences between the two statements, and I had her listen to and feel the difference. You can try it too, right now. Say each sentence out loud, and see if you can feel the difference. Hint: you *can* feel a difference. The first statement is ambiguous, and might be interpreted in several ways. The second is clear: The patient (who, btw, was struggling to know what she wanted, in life, in relationships, in work. And for dessert. Hell, she struggled to know what she wanted to eat. I suggested a Norwegian meal.) was able to feel the difference. And it was a great start on her learning to listen to herself, and learn what she wanted.

That was long. Hopefully it was clear. If not, well....You may need to see a therapist to help with that clarity.

The Skill of Statements, 2.0

We humans are funny creatures. We can be so amazing. We have created so much beauty, we are responsible for so much innovation. We can also be so destructive, always to our own disadvantage.

This capacity for destruction is not just in big matters... wars, environmental destruction, extinction, hairdos of the '50's... it is in small matters as well. Especially, it is in individual matters, in our interpersonal relationships and most importantly, in our relationship with ourself.

As humans, we have a need for socialization, some to a greater extent, some less so. The continuum of healthy socialization is very broad, so most of us fit within that healthy spectrum. No matter the degree of socialization we need, all of us are extremely competent at making a mess of it.

Why is this?! What is wrong with us, that we have such a strong urge for others, and yet can make such a disaster and disappointment of relationships? Well, first: there's nothing *wrong* with us. We as humans are incredibly, indescribably complex and so we have a number of wants and urges going on at any one moment. Second: as humans, we are survivalist creatures...

Interruption here!

Stuhlism #6

Humans are survivalist creatures. We always, *always* choose an option that we believe helps us. We may not initially see how it benefits us, but deep within our minds, there is a belief or set of beliefs that support our choice as one that helps us. Examples to come later.

... and now, back to survivalist creatures. We mess up relationships because we become fearful for our inner self, of hurt to our emotional, psychological self. And so, we act in ways to protect ourself. And one such way is that we *often ask questions when we're really making a statement*. Once more, here are some examples.

Question: Do you really believe I would do that to you?
Statement: I promise, I did not do that to you.
Better yet: I promise, I am faithful to you. (See! It's free of negatives!)

Question: You don't really want to go to the beach, do you?
Statement: I don't want to go to the beach this year.
Better yet: I want to vacation somewhere different this summer. (Again, free of negatives!)

It didn't hurt that bad, did it?
Statement: I believe you are okay. You sure seem to be okay.

The significance of questions being used rather than statements is that a question, unless it is for information, is a passive form of communication. When we ask a question but we're really trying to communicate something, we are hiding ourselves. And this almost always causes confusion on the part of the other. And confusion, unless specifically addressed and clarified, leads to more confusion, which then leads to hurt feelings, misunderstandings, emotional distance, frustration, anger and finally, the ruination of all life and a failure of the laws of the universe. Well, hopefully not *quite* that far.

"But what's the skill, Dr. J?" The skill is this: listen to yourself, and ask a question *only* when you need information. Otherwise, figure out what you are actually stating, and make a statement. Preferably using "I Language".

I had a supervisor once, long ago, named A. Kempton Haynes. In every group and individual supervision session, Dr. Haynes would say, "Every question has a hook on the end of it," and he would make a little air hook with his pinkie. "Don't try to hook people; let them off the hook, and just share with them what you want to say." It was really helpful for me to learn this. I did ask, "What if I am actually needing information, as when I'm doing a psychological assessment of a patient?" His answer was, "Wonder about things, John. Share with the person what you *wonder* about." Then he added, "And just then, John? You hooked me. Ouch."

Yeah, he was a little extreme. And yet, what he was teaching has been very, very helpful for me through the years.

Okay, enough for now on this language thing. There's probably more of it to come, but my brain just froze up, and so let's move on to something fun. But as we go, here's another little package of delight.

Stuhlism #7

Humans have the absolute right to totally and completely fuck up their lives. And we can't stop them, no matter how hard we try, or how badly we want to.

I'll blather on about that somewhere further on.

On Trauma

"Wait a minute, John, you said 'on to fun stuff'. What the hell's fun about trauma?!"

You know what? You are correct. We'll look at trauma later. How about some fun facts instead?

Stuhlism #8

When dealing with others, 97.8 percent of the time, in the research (I made up in my mind), *it has nothing to do with you!*

We get so caught up in ourselves that when we interact with other people, and there is some confusion or hurt, frustration or anger, some judgment or criticism, we think it means something about us, about what we're doing. Especially if the other person is not practicing the skills identified above, and is telling us "You were so mean to me!...You are so insensitive!....No one can understand you!...This is all your fault!" Or any other such nonsense.

I've shared the following example with most of you. However, I know that because I talk so much in therapy, you may have become inured to my voice. So, here is the example again, to model the above mentioned Stuhlism.

I have provided therapy for Ms. Eda May Drummel for six sessions. At the seventh session, Ms. Drummel says the following:

"Dr. Stuhl, I'm going to stop therapy. I actually don't ever want to see you again, or hear from you again. If you happen to see me out in public, please don't even acknowledge that I'm there. I don't want to know you, or anyone who is related to you, or even any of your friends. The reason is, you are so sacrilegious, God is going to send you to hell, and everyone who cares about you to hell also. Goodbye."

Now, I could get very offended by this…"I'm a professional, you old biddy, don't talk to me that way." Or, I could get really hurt and upset…"What did I say that was so offensive? How was I so insensitive to this sweet lady?" Or, I could get really angry…"No one ever talks to me that way, Ms. Wretched Life Waste. I am a Doctor! And a Minister! How dare you think you know better than me about theology and psychology! You are fired as a patient, and I'm double billing you, for failure as a human and a Christian. Or Muslim. Wiccan. Whatever you are." However, if I've believed my own statistic above, I am free to respond without any emotion at all, with detachment. Why? Because I know Mrs. Drummel's attitudes and perspectives *have nothing to do with me!* They say nothing about me; they mean nothing about me. Mrs. Drummel's attitudes and beliefs say something *about her!* Her beliefs are about her own narrow attitudes, about her being critical and judgmental of others, about her small mindedness, about her fears.

Here is the real irony: Mrs. Drummel is absolutely, positively 100% correct. I am sacrilegious! I am intentionally so (my apologies to those of you who are deity committed). For me, being sacrilegious is healthy. It's also fun. What is true for me is that a lot of our dysfunctional, harmful beliefs come from religion…yes, I know religion and god/faith are not the same thing. However, all too often, they get mashed together and for many people are indistinguishable. For me, sacrilege is healthy. (And if god doesn't like it, she can come down and we'll have a chat about it. But otherwise, she can hush and hang around somewhere else and we humans will take care of things). This is true for me. It is my truth.

Because I am comfortable with this truth, I have no insecurities or doubts about it. Because I am secure about my belief about sacrilegious-ness, when Mrs. Drummel makes statements that are damning, critical, and judgmental, I am unphased. I have no emotional reaction to it (except maybe bemusement), because, as I keep saying, *it has nothing to do with me!*

So, when we have emotional reactions to something said to us or about us, it suggests that *we* have some insecurity or angst or anxiety about ourselves. Which leads us to two more Stuhlisms.

Stuhlism #9

What is true for me, may not be true for you or someone else.

Another way to say this is:

Find what is true for you, believe what is true for you, and live by your own truths, not anyone else's.

I love examples, though I realize that each example can have exceptions and potentially cause confusion rather than clarity. Yet, I love examples, so here's another one.

It has been very clearly determined (by the scholars who do such work and research) that since humans evolved (we're still saying "evolved," though there is evidence to suggest that humans "devolved" from hominids), a portion of the human population has been homosexual. Up until about fifty years ago, society did not accept homosexuality as "normal." In fact, it was considered a "sin" by religions (Still is, with some. Shame on them.), abnormal or an illness by the field of medicine, and simply wrong and repulsive by society in general. Homosexuals were forced into lives of lies. They had to hide who they were for fear of persecution or worse.

But that didn't make true what society/heterosexuals said was "true." Attraction to the opposite sex was what was acceptable, normal. And yet, it wasn't—not for homosexuals.

Thank whatever deities involved (if any) that most of society has moved past such abhorrent thinking. People's sexual orientations are accepted (mostly, or to put it more succinctly, accepted by anyone who holds healthy beliefs about sexual orientation—which means, yes, criticism, judgement, and rejection of another's sexual orientation is an unhealthy, dysfunctional belief).

The point of this example is that what is true for one group of people is not true for another. What is true for me, may not be true for you. What is true for you may not be true for me. In fact, what is true for you may not be true for anyone else! However, if that's the case, I suggest you see a psychologist and do a little reality testing.

Stuhlism #10

There are no "should's."

This one is mind boggling for most of us. "What the hell? There are no "should's"? Well, shouldn't there be?"

See, it happens so quickly. So unconsciously. Expansion on this concept may help.   First expansion. There are no "should's." There are no "ought's." There are no "have to's," "must's," no "shall's," no "gotta be's."

There are no absolute rules given from above that we "have to" obey, adhere to, live by.

Second expansion. "John, your first expansion is causing me to have major brain cramps.
What about morals, John? What about what god wants us to do? What about the ten commandments? Jesus' teachings? The laws of our city, or county, or country? What about what our spouse says we have to do?"

There are so many rules, laws, edicts, should's that we have unconsciously assimilated in our lives, and that lie within our mind, just below the surface or deep within our unconscious, that Stuhlism #10 is difficult to accept. And, of course, you don't have to! Remember, what's true for me may not be true for you. But if you'll grant me a moment or two, I'll explain this Stuhlism.

Why would I say there are no "should's"? How can I say this? Here are the reasons.

All social structures in our lives are created by humans; if we're really candid about it, they were created by males because females had little voice five and ten thousand years ago. Almost all societies were patriarchal, and it was mostly males who were in power.

"But what about the Bible, John, you hell-bound heathen! Maybe Mrs. Drummel had a point."

Well, let's look at the Bible. Within the religion of Christianity, the Bible is considered "the word of god." But how did we get that? There are all kinds of declarations: Moses went up on Mount Sinai and God gave him the ten commandments; Jesus taught his followers, and they recorded his teachings; the prophets and apostles and leaders of the church were inspired by god in what they wrote; Joseph Smith was instructed by god to dig in his backyard and find invisible golden plates.

All great concepts. All great analogies. However...

Whomever it was that received whatever message they received, they still had to record it in some fashion. And, we who hear these teachings and ideas today, *still have to choose to believe what is said, or taught, or read!* It is still up to us to decide what is real and what to grant authority to.

"Woah, ho, Dr. J! Now we've got you! What you're saying is that unless we believe it, it isn't real! That's small thinking, Dr. J; in fact, it's so sad, we're taking your 'Dr.' away."

That's not quite what I'm saying. There are realities that exist apart from us, and we would be foolish not to attend to them. For example, we may choose not to believe in gravity, but gravity is still going to believe in us, so if we jump off a skyscraper, crying "Gravity's not real! I defy gravity!",

gravity's gonna say, "Okay, you can defy me… for about seven seconds."

I am not saying that nothing exists apart from what we believe (though there are some philosophers who seem to go that far). What I am saying, especially with regards to the structures of human society and human interactions, that our belief in a rule or law is what gives it power in our life.

You'd like an example, I'm sure. Okay, here's one.

For eons, there has been the belief that any sex other than sex within marriage (and a marriage between a man and a wife, no less), was improper, immoral, wrong. Against god's will. You know what? There are eight billion people on our space rock, and I doubt more than 3.2% believe that anymore—I had to factor fundamentalist, evangelical Christians in this calculation. This belief has changed for the vast majority of people. Most simply do not believe what was once believed by so many (Or at least, so many *said* that's what they believed! So many of them sure didn't adhere to the belief.)

The point of all this meandering is that when we struggle in relationships, with ourselves or others, we are so often struggling against unconscious and subconscious beliefs that we no longer hold true. By identifying there are no "should's" or any of "should's'" cousins, we can begin to examine the beliefs we do have, and choose which beliefs are true for us.

Let me give a second example. We've all grown up with some form of idea of "family first." "Blood is thicker than water." "You always stand by your family." "Never let your family down." "You have to love your family."

The intent behind these beliefs is admirable. However, what happens if a young girl is sexually molested by her father habitually, for years, until she is able to escape at the age of 17? Should she "honor her father"? Should she always put her father first?

Of course not. She needs to heal her wounds from such trauma and evil (and her wounds can be healed), but she doesn't have to keep her father in her life. In fact, she may want to never see him again. She may choose to see him as nothing more than "a donor." She may even choose another person to look at as her father, a surrogate to whom she will always turn when she needs an older male's support or care or guidance.

Here's an associated Stuhlism.

Stuhlism #11

You, become god of your own life.

One of my goals in therapy is to help people become god of their own lives.

"You're getting out there, John. You've already lost your "Dr.", you're about to lose your mind."

Oh, I don't think so. I support most anything a person wants to believe, as long as it's healthy and generally legal, and not harmful or dysfunctional. What I mean by becoming god of your own life is that you get to decide what your life will be. No one else. Not even a god (if she's really out there). What I want for you, and what I work for, is for you to find what is true *for you*. To listen to yourself; to hear your own truths that come from deep within you. Your truths. Your life. You are the creator of your life: you and you alone. When we embrace this factoid, this Stuhlism, we take powerful control of our own healing. And we become the creator of our life.

Stuhlism #12

We resonate with our truth.

As I said before, healing is the process of tracking pain. When we arrive at the sources of pain, where our wounds are, we don't just *feel* those feelings. Our goal is to *heal* those painful feelings. That healing occurs when we determine what beliefs maintain the pain, and shift or change or simply dismiss those beliefs. Before I explain, let me give an essential accompanying belief.

Stuhlism #13

Painful feelings, emotional hurts, are maintained by negative beliefs.

This may be one of the most important discoveries I've ever made. I wasn't the originator of this factoid; it was someone else whose name isn't important (because I can't remember it). For me, this is one very, very powerful factoid. Possibly the most powerful factoid. In fact, it is so powerful and important, it is possibly even a fact!

Now, to explain, and hopefully to capture the concept of the preceding Stuhlism as well.

It is my personal and professional belief that humans are born with an innate sense of justice, an innate self-worth and value. Life fights to exist, to live. Why? How do I know? All of life fights to survive. While I can't say why that is, my interpretation of this is that all life values its existence. Let's stick with humans, because you and I are humans (I know: a big assumption on my part!) and we can understand this best if we look at ourselves. The youngest human, an infant, wants to be fed, comforted, soothed, held, and made to feel safe and secure. The infant doesn't actually *think* this; it is just part of the hard wiring that comes with the package. And when an infant doesn't get one of these needs met, when the infant is hungry or scared or wet or suffering listening to rap music, the infant lets us know her discomfort. She cries. She fusses. Why is that? Because that infant wants what she wants. She wants what she needs. She values her life not because she *thinks* that, but simply because the self-value is there. Life values itself. So, a life—your life, my life—has an innate sense of self-value and worth.

If we accept this belief (and I'll expound on it more in another chapter), then we can extrapolate. When a child gets what she or he needs, the child is soothed, the child is satisfied, and on a most basic level, the child is made happy. The child feels happiness.

Healthy states are created and maintained by positive gifts and experiences; painful states occur when there is a lack of something needed, which I would describe as a negative experience.

What's true for us as infants is also true for us throughout our life, but it becomes infinitely more complicated. Why? Because of our damn brains! As we grow, we begin to live out of our beliefs. Our minds, which are so magnificent, are also the reservoir of a ton of our troubles.

Stuhlism #14

Our psyches, our emotional, psychological self, bends towards healing just as our physical bodies bend towards health.

Let's take the physical first...which I guess means we're getting physical. <Cue Olivia Newton John's classic video> Should we suffer a cut, say, on our right thigh approximately seven centimeters above the knee (yes, I can be a little OCD), immediately our body goes into survival and healing mode. First, we grab the spot where we're cut—and actually, we do this fractions of a second before we feel the pain, because pressure travels faster than pain along our nerves. Second, the command centers in our brains immediately send out coagulants to stop the bleeding. Also, white blood cells are dispatched to fight infection. New skin cells begin to regenerate almost immediately.

All of this is done without our having to do a thing. Our unconscious takes care of all of it; it's one of the autonomic processes, just like heart rate, respiration, body temperature control, and the instantaneous capacity to locate chocolate anywhere within a seven meter radius. And, it is an indication of how our physical self bends towards healing.

As with the physical, so too the emotional, psychological self. When we suffer some emotional pain or hurt, we have processes and mechanisms built into our brain and mind that begin the healing. As I said earlier, this cognitive structure has been called the Adaptive Information Processing Capacity, and because I like that term a lot, I'll keep using it. Let's say we suffer an emotional wound: a friend of ours betrays a trust we shared with him, and then lies about disclosing it and turns around and criticizes us, and rejects us.

A number of hurts in this experience, right? We may feel devastated. We may feel embarrassed, or worse, ashamed at our secret being known by others. We will almost certainly feel hurt, and anger. There are a host of emotions we are very likely to have, any one of which, if it has enough intensity, might overwhelm us to the point where we might feel defeated or destroyed.

And yet, almost none of us die from such an experience. Instead, our brain may produce shock, so that the intensity of feelings is muted. Our mind may start immediately thinking about how we are going to remove this person from our life (possibly even how we're going to remove this person from life), how we are going to respond to a friend's intrusive or concerned questions. We may unconsciously begin to identify beliefs that help to reduce our sense of shame or embarrassment.

All of this activity can, and most often does, occur without our conscious, intentional efforts. It is as if our mind wants to heal the painful emotions, because, well…it does want to heal them. Keeping painful emotions serves no purpose. Of course, just like physical wounds, emotional wounds take time to heal. Which reminds me.

Stuhlism # 15

Time doesn't heal shit.

We've all heard the old adage: time heals all wounds. Well, yeah—bullshit. Time doesn't heal shit. How do I know? Because I've worked with patients whose wounds occurred years, sometimes decades, ago. And the wounds are still there. The pain and the anguish are still as intense, still as debilitating as they were when they occurred.

What I can say about time is that some wounds will require a length of time to heal. Any parent who has suffered the tragedy of their child's death will take at least a year to heal fully. Why? Because the grieving parent has a whole year of firsts to endure: going through the first Christmas without the child; the child's birthday; the first extended family gathering without the child present. There are so many firsts in that first year that no parent can fully heal in that time. It's just impossible.

So, time has a part to play in our healing. But what really brings about the healing of our emotional pain is our mind's capacity and drive to heal, to be well. Which leads my thoughts to…

Stuhlism #16

Our brains crave balance.

As we heal, we unlock a great deal of emotional energy. We free it to be put to use in much more meaningful, fulfilling, creative ways other than just suppressing our painful feelings. When our emotional hurts and pains are unresolved, unhealed, our mind is out of balance. Our minds search for balance, lean towards balance, yearn for balance, and they are healthier when we are able to achieve psychological, emotional balance.

All of this—our minds bending towards health, our minds craving balance, unresolved hurts and emotional pain taking intentional efforts to heal if our natural processes are unable to complete the healing—all of this is to add emphasis to our own healing efforts. For, you see, when we actively seek to heal our emotional hurts, *we are working in tandem with our mind's natural desire and direction!* Our mind wants healing;

when we are active in our healing process our efforts are empowered and enhanced by what our mind already seeks.

Now, that's hopeful. Incredibly hopeful. In fact, it is the reason that I believe almost every emotional pain and hurt can be healed. I can't say "all," because I'm averse to using absolutes. But if I were to use an absolute, this would be one of the places: I do believe that all emotional hurts can heal. Of course, the healing may not look like what we had imagined, but that's another matter.

I just reread all of that, from Stuhlism #9 down, and wow! That was long. And a long way from the elucidation of Stuhlism #9. Let me save you looking it up: *We resonate with our truth.* (My editor, whom you may feel on quite the personal level with by now, had this to add: "I've heard this idea of something resonating with us referred to as 'ringing the chime of truth,' within ourselves, which I like very much." I like that very much too. It makes me feel like I may be smart, like real psychologists and writers.)

The significance of this Stuhlism is that as we learn to listen to ourselves, healthy beliefs will stand out.

How do we know what are our truths?

My chuckling answer is, "Ask me."

But that's just joking around. The way we know what our truths are is *we learn to listen to ourselves.* And, as I'm sure most of you are aware from our sessions together, listening to ourself, hearing our own voice, is not easy. It is difficult; it can be very, very difficult. So let me talk about why.

Remember earlier when I was saying that humans have an innate sense of self-worth and self-value? And that this innate value in each of us is what drives us to seek healing, because we inherently know we deserve it? Well, a reasonable question then is why don't we all heal, quickly and without resistance? Why don't we all seek healing right away? Why don't we seek help to heal immediately when we become aware of our hurts? Why does healing become so complicated? Well, to repeat myself, it is because of our damn brains. Our minds, which are so magnificent, are also the reservoir of a ton of our troubles.

As infants, we live out of our basic, fundamental drives and desires. But we as humans are thinking creatures. (Well, most of us are. However, I won't list the exceptions here—I want this to be less than 70,000 words). Our brains crave information. Our minds crave knowledge. And from the moment we are born, our magnificent brains and minds are absorbing information and knowledge at a miraculous rate.

As we grow, we shift from living out of our fundamental drives and desires, to *living out of our knowledge!*

And that knowledge comes to us in a myriad of fashions (feelings expressed to us from others, messages and teachings from parents, siblings, teachers, leaders of churches and day cares and organizations like Girl Scouts and AmericaCorp and Sons of the Confederacy; stories and books and movies and Big Bird; playmates and teammates and the troublemaker who lived thee blocks over). We are inundated with beliefs and thoughts and teachings of how we "should" live and what we "should" believe and what is "true for everybody."

Do you think there is great consistency in the messages and beliefs we are taught? You are correct: according to the research (that I made up in my mind, but at another time than the one mentioned before), there is a lot of consistency. On the basics. But when we move from global messages…"Wash your hands, germs will kill you," "Let's keep our hands to ourselves; hitting is not nice," "Don't chew with your mouth open," "Double dipping is detestable"…when we move away from the large, global messages, we receive uncountable conflicting messages. "Don't hit others." "It's okay to protect yourself." "When you're on the football field, you hit someone as hard as you can." "The strong survive." "Aggressiveness is next to godliness."

We absorb boodles and bazillions of inconsistent, contradictory beliefs. And this is what makes healing emotional wounds so difficult, because emotional wounds are sustained by negative beliefs, and we have eighty bazillion beliefs stuck in our subconscious and unconscious, many of them absolutely contradictory. And we don't hear them! Those beliefs are there, under the surface, and because they attach to emotional pains and psychological hurts, those beliefs unwittingly sustain the pains that we want to heal.

And it is hard, hard work to dig up our cognitions and root out the unhealthy ones. Why? Because the beliefs, even if they are unhealthy, are still familiar. They have longevity. They have established a pattern of presence, and won't go willingly into the void. Which leads me to another whimsical thought…

Stuhlism #17

Our brain develops habits, and thoughts become habits, even unhealthy and dysfunctional thoughts and beliefs.

So when we begin the healing of our emotional pains and hurts, we are often working against our own mind. A brain which is the most complex organ in the universe that we know of. It is more complex than the fastest supercomputers. In fact, it has been written that the mind of an earthworm is more intelligent than the fastest supercomputer because of the earthworm's ability to adapt and adjust to the environment. And if that's true for an earthworm, think what that says about human brains. I am making the assumption here that all human brains are superior to any and every earthworm brain. But it's only an assumption.

Fun factoid--a brain neuron has connection contacts (synapses) to a thousand other neurons; there are approximately one hundred *billion* neurons in the brain, and there are over sixty neuro-transmitters in the brain.

Think what kind of number that makes. Calculate the combinations of one hundred billion neurons with one thousand synaptic connections each and each synapse has over sixty neurotransmitters active. The combination potentials are, well, ginormous.

Back to our damn brains. Yes, healing can be difficult because there is so much complexity in our thoughts and beliefs. We have beliefs about beliefs, beliefs about emotions, beliefs about choices, and they can be one convoluted mess. Finding our way through that mess, and then having the will and courage to change our beliefs, is a huge challenge. Huge! And yet, it can be done.

Another factoid. Therapy is for healing.

The goal of therapy is not simply to uncover emotional wounds and help a person feel them (that would be stupid). The goal is to find those wounds, identify the painful emotions that are trapped there, and *help those wounds to heal.* And a huge part, maybe the most significant part, of healing wounds is the resolving of painful feelings, which may involve feeling those feelings for the first time, but must involve changing the negative beliefs that sustain the pain.

I'm getting tired of factoids, probably because I can't think of any more right now. Are you tired of them? Yes? So let's shift to something new, and if more come into my mind, I'll throw those into the next chapters.

Don't Be a But Head

No, that's not a misspelling. But, maybe it'd be better if I put it this way.

Don't Be a "But" Head

That better? Great.

Now, what does that mean?

I'm confident I've shared this with almost all of you. If so, you can skip the rest of this short chapter and head on to the next. Or, if you'd like a refresher, read on.

There is nothing wrong with the word "but." It's a multi-talented little bugger: it can be a preposition, an adverb, a noun or a conjunction. And, it is this last usage that I focus on, because the word 'but' as a conjunction in human speech and interaction is trouble. This kind of "but" is a verbal eraser.

Let's start with an example.

A husband says to his wife of thirty-seven years, "You know, Gladys, I am so lucky to be married to you (in spite of your first name). We've been married thirty-seven years, and I still look at you and see a beautiful, sexy woman. I still get excited to come home. I still am thrilled to have time together. And my life would be a total wreck without you. But you look like you've gained a little weight."

And his wife hears, "I'm fat." And the husband is a dead man.

All those compliments, erased. All that love, dismissed. All because of the little word "but."

This happens to us so often when we are working through difficulties in a relationship. A husband and wife are arguing, and she says, "Look, I'm sorry for yelling." And he responds, "I appreciate your apology, but I still don't understand why you were yelling." And his wife's apology, given genuinely, is dismissed. Her effort to make a connection (because that's what genuine apologies do) is cast aside. Even if her husband didn't mean to dismiss her, he did. That's what we as humans experience when we are "but-ed" this way.

Think about the disagreements you've had with someone you love. Think about ongoing arguments that don't get resolved but are simply pushed aside, or dropped, never to be picked back up. Listen to yourself in your conversations with your significant others, whomever they may be. Hear the word "but" and pay attention to what happens to the exchange when "buts" start appearing.

Probably something similar to a disagreement if "butts" start appearing. Hahahaha—I made a joke here! I funny!

And if you want to make a change, and find ways to eliminate buts, practice how you can say the same sentence without it. Listen to how you express the two messages, because there are two messages in a sentence with "but" in it: a message in the first half of the sentence, before the "but," and the message after. Here are some examples.

> You say you love me, but you bought that boat without even asking me.
> Changed to…
> You say you love me. And you bought that boat without even asking me.

Or

> I really want to go hiking with you, but I still have all this work to do.
> Changed to . . .
> I really want to go hiking with you. I still all this work to do.

Or

> I appreciate your saying that, but it still doesn't explain your actions.
> Changed to . . .
> I appreciate your saying that. I still don't understand your actions.

As you read these three pairs, spend a little time with them. Try reading them out loud. Pay attention to how you feel as you say each one. The second statement in each of these pairs is so much more open. The second statements allow for more understanding and exploration, while the first statements actually evoke defensiveness.

This is true for language itself; it is vastly more true in speech, for when we are talking, discussing, arguing, sharing, resolving a conflict, we communicate so much more than just our words.

We all know this. Reminders help, though. Here are two reminders I use to help myself when communicating with people.

1. Studies have shown (and these are real studies, not just the ones I've conducted in my mind) that seventy percent of emotional, affective communication is non-verbal. Seventy percent! That's 70%! Technically speaking, that's called "a whole bunch," or "Twenty percent more than fifty percent!" So, when we're resolving a conflict (hopefully not arguing), a 'but' is very powerful, because it most often comes with a great deal of emotion. Which means, we are powerfully erasing someone at an emotional, psychological level. When we "but" someone, it is often experienced as a negation, as a dismissal of the other. This is almost never our intent; however, it is what is experienced. Most "buts" are experienced as

defensive, and when we are being defensive, the other person does not feel heard or valued; the other person experiences that his or her concern is of less importance than our concern.

2. There are two parts to our communication: pragmatics and semantics. Pragmatics are the actual words we use. Semantics are the message we are delivering. And these can be exactly opposite! This is the role sarcasm, mockery, and irony play in communication.

It is difficult to give an example of the difference between pragmatics and semantics, but let me try.

First, hear in your mind this statement being said with tenderness and real affection. "You know I love you more than I love anyone else." Ah, that's sweet, isn't it? That sounds (and more importantly, feels) so loving. I'm grateful I get to hear that from time to time from my wife. Well, I'm glad I've heard it twice.

Second, hear in your mind this statement being spoken with a voice that drips sarcasm. "You know I love *you* more than I love anyone else." Ouch, that stings. Right?! (I added the italics to help with our hearing.) Same statement, same pragmatics; absolutely opposite semantics, opposite meaning.

I realize I've transitioned from simply talking about "buts" and started yammering more broadly about communication. So, let me jump to the next chapter, and leave this one with the simple adage: "Don't be a but head."

However! My recommendation to improve our communication by removing buts does have a qualifier. We can't remove "buts" from our communications completely (we don't have to be perfect at any of this <in fact, I'll wander onto that subject in just a minute>). And there are actually ways we can use "but" to good advantage. One more adaptation to the "but" example above. Here's the original presentation of the statement.

> "I appreciate your apology, but I still don't understand why."
> Changed to...
> "I still don't understand why (you did what you did). But I appreciate your apology."

See? Now I've actually enhanced my acceptance of the apology. This is good. So, maybe instead of just saying "Don't be a 'but head'," I oughta say "Be judicious with your 'buts'."

Communication Assisters

"Dr. J, you were focused on healing, then wandered off into communication. What's up with that?"

Great question. While healing is something that we do internally, and that only we can do for ourselves, many of our struggles in life are the result of conflicts with others. The more we can pay attention to the way we communicate, and what we communicate, the more effective and influential a person we become, and the more we can evoke from life that which we want. The more we are very intentional and skilled at our communications, the healthier and more satisfying are our relations. And who doesn't want their relationships to be warmer, closer, more loving and caring? Most of us. However, you are correct if you thought, "Well, there are some people who don't want to improve their relationships, or who don't care about the quality of their relationships." So true. Of course, we can say that such people are pretty disturbed and could use therapy, a *whole lot of therapy*. However, they'll probably never get therapy, because they don't care. The people in their orbit will get therapy, though!

So, part of our healing is learning how to better get along with others, and one way we do this is by improving our communications. To do that, guidelines are helpful. These are some guidelines I've developed that have definitely helped me.

Make statements instead of asking questions. Was this covered earlier? I think so; I'll go back and check.

Slow our speech. When we are working through a conflict, we tend to get emotional, and we start to speak faster. If we slow our speech, we invite more discussion and less argument.

Soften our voice. Goes right along with slower speech. As emotions rise, our voice gets louder. The reverse is generally true as well; as we raise the volume of our speech, others experience more intense emotions in us and tend to match us in intensity. And there is an upward spiral of contention.

If the other's voice gets loud, use that as an indicator to lower our own voice. We tend to match another's intensity and volume when discussions degrade into arguments. When we succumb to this understandable unconscious reaction, we simply increase degrees of separation and the difficulty of resolution. But if we can train ourselves to use the increase in volume and intensity as a signal to ourselves, we can be the agents of change and reconciliation in our circles of influence.

Speak in short statements. What I have witnessed, and fallen prey too, is that we often make very long and winding statements to the one with whom we're struggling. We share a thought or perspective, then give several examples to prove our point, and unconsciously realize that in our examples are several other thoughts and opinions we want to share, so we go ahead and share those, then add the necessary examples to prove *those* points, and on it goes, much like this sentence. By the time we're finished, whomever we're speaking to is either so frustrated at having to wait five hours to respond, or so overwhelmed with all they've heard, that they don't know how to respond. So, when they get the chance, they jump in with their own reservoir of thoughts, and their communications are influenced by their own heightened emotions. Before you know it, there is a battle of epic-length diatribes, and everyone loses. Solution? Learn to speak in very short sentences, very short phrases…and then pause. Don't talk. Stop. Wait. And let the other speak.

Ensure the other has heard us correctly. This is simple, but simplicity has not made this skill more prevalent. Make a short statement, or share in brief what you think or feel, and then ask, "What did you hear me say?" It's that simple. I say to my friend, "I was really upset that I haven't heard from you," then ask, "What did you hear me say?" and my friend answers "You hate me when I don't text back immediately." Well, noooo, that's not what I said, and it wasn't what I wanted to communicate.

When we practice this skill, even though it can feel cumbersome, our arguments become discussions, and our conflicts become exercises in understanding and respect.

Stay with a single communication until clarity has been reached, until you are accurately heard, or the other feels accurately heard. This accompanies the short statements and checks-for-understanding. In the example above, I might respond to the "You hate me when I don't text back immediately..." with "I'm sorry. That's not what I wanted to communicate. I wanted you to know I get worried about you when I don't hear back from you within a reasonable time, like, say....Twelve hours." Maybe I wish I'd said that first; but maybe I needed to slow down and have a check to see for myself what I was really trying to say. When we get immediate feedback on what the other has heard, it helps *us* to clarify what *we* are wanting to communicate. So, this skill is helpful to the other, and to ourselves, for clarity.

Simply accept responsibility. In the example above, I began my clarification with "I'm sorry...." What I have discovered is that it is easier and much more effective if, when someone has misunderstood me, I accept that I wasn't clear in my communication, *not* insist that "they didn't hear me correctly." If it is the other who is misunderstanding, then it is as if I'm criticizing or blaming them. And this almost always evokes defensiveness. If I accept responsibility for the misunderstanding, I lower my friend's defensiveness (well, hopefully), I invite better listening, and I am communicating to my friend that this issue/conflict/disagreement is not all their fault. I am not looking to place blame on them; I am looking to understand them. Does that make sense? Hope so, though do remember, if you answer yes, you may be defying the laws of nature, as I am an old, white male—we as a species rarely make sense.

Speak one at a time. This seems obvious, and yet, I am constantly amazed how two or three people, especially when working through a conflict or disagreement, lose touch with this skill. Time after time, when working with couples or families or friends in a session, I find myself saying "Both of you are talking at the same time." Usually what I get in response is…surprise. They didn't even realize they were doing that. Both or all were so caught up in what they wanted to *say* that they had no room or space to *hear*! Once pointed out though, and with just a small amount of effort, this habit can be broken.

Use "I" Language. I have mentioned this earlier, and I'll look to see if I droned on about it enough. I will just add here: the more we can talk and share about ourselves, i.e. use "I" statements, the more we open dialogue to communication and understanding, and away from arguments and conflicts. Shifts can be this simple.

"You are always yelling at me!" (Notice the absolute that comes with the word "always" as well.)

Becomes…

"I feel yelled at." If I'm really on my game and working hard to understand, I might add,
"Are you yelling? Do you feel like you are yelling, because maybe I'm just being extra sensitive." Okay, truth here—I've probably never said that, but read it in a book somewhere. I doubt I've ever been that good at communicating. I believe my wife can validate my assessment.

SELF DISCLOSURE: I am somewhat of a therapeutic, communication eunuch— I can tell you what to do and how to do it, but I can't always do it myself. In other words, in my conversations I can fail miserably in the practice of skills I believe in and promote. I'm not perfect with these skills (don't need to be—more on that in a bit), but I keep trying.

Back to skills.

Let our emotions be expressed, and felt. A caveat: not necessarily our more difficult emotions, like anger, irritation, annoyance, hostility—these are probably already getting expressed, if we're dealing with some conflict. I mean the more sensitive emotions, like hurt, care, concern, distress, worry. When we express these emotions when working through conflicts, we allow ourselves to be seen more. The other person can feel and experience that we are not just out to get them or blame them; we want to find understanding and resolution. When we allow these emotions to be expressed, the other feels our love and connection, and usually, this evokes more empathy and efforts to understand on their part.

When at all possible, always speak directly to the person. I see this more in therapy, when I'm working with couples or families, or a group. Let's say it's marriage counseling: I will ask one person what they've heard, or as my persnickety editor might say, I've asked the one partner to directly express to the other what they understood from the communication, and instead of addressing their partner, they talk to me, *about their partner.* It's as if the partner isn't even there. I understand this pattern; it is much more risky and self-disclosing to talk directly to someone than it is to talk about them to a third party. And sometimes, this can actually be helpful in resolving conflicts or hurt. There are times when the partner being referred to is actually able to be one step removed, and can hear with less defensiveness. Usually, however, it is most beneficial to talk to the other person, not about them.

Find our own patterns. We all of us have patterns that have developed in our communications. One of my own is I tend to look for, see, and identify the healthy emotions and positive aspects of a circumstance. This has led to there being times when the other person doesn't feel their pain is heard, or given validation. I have been told that I didn't make room for the person's painful feelings. In therapist jargon, that is called…"bad therapist." I understand why I do this: I want to help people heal. I want to help the person find the skills and strategies that help to resolve their painful feelings. And I forget that a part of healing is for me to simply be present with someone as they express whatever their pain is, to not be afraid of their pain, and to sit with them as they experience it. I have a tendency to believe that the person has known and lived with their pain for a long time, and what is most important is that we bring healing to their pain, not simply become entrapped in the experiencing of it.

Let me identify some of the common patterns I find that frustrate and inhibit healing conversations and interactions.

A tendency to say "No" as a first response. I have a patient (Remember, all patient examples are mash-ups. If you find yourself in one of the examples, IT IS NOT YOU. It is simply that you can resonate with that example. This is important, both for your comfort and for my liability.) Back to…I have a patient. As we worked together, I realized how frequently she used the word "No." Often, she used it as a conjunction, a transition word. Still, I realized its effect on me; that I would get frustrated hearing it, because I frequently felt negated. At the beginning of one session, I shared the pattern I'd noticed, and asked the patient if it felt accurate for her. She recognized the pattern (and she was pretty pissed with herself, because she was working so hard at communicating more effectively with her children and husband), and asked me to "catch her" during session. So, I did. I began to count the "No's" and to simply say, "There's another one, Delilah." I'd hear back, "Well, shit!"

During one session, I shared with her about one special interaction I had with my younger brother Glenn, a time that was very touching to me. Delilah began her immediate response with "No, no, no, no, no!", and quickly added how much love she felt I expressed for Glenn. I then simply said, "One. Two. Three. Four. Five." And Delilah responded with "God dammit! I appreciate you too much to negate you, Dr. J."

I was very touched; many say I am touched, but that's another matter. I knew the very close connection between Delilah and me; I was certain of the bond we shared. In fact, it was one of the reasons I could share as I did. The happy result is that Delilah almost completely eliminated "No's" from her responses, especially her initial responses to someone. And she almost always caught herself when she did start with a "No," and would change it to "Oh." Her change was endearing, the emotional distance she was experiencing in her relationships was transcended, and she began to feel and express the affection she had for her loved ones, and felt theirs as well.

A tendency to be defensive. To defend ourselves is normal and natural. It is actually a healthy trait, when used at the right times and with prudence. However, when we are working through conflicts, defensiveness is almost always counterproductive. Noticing our defensiveness can be a challenge; I find I notice mine more effectively if my first response is to either explain myself, give examples of how I am right, or begin talking about the other person and what they are doing wrong or thinking wrong. If we can catch our defensiveness, we can greatly increase the quality of our relationships.

A tendency to be passive, and to quickly accept the blame, or agree the problem is all ours. I am not talking about healthy acceptance of responsibility. I am talking about immediate, unremittent self-blame and self-criticism. When we engage in this behavior, we struggle to build healthy relationships, because *we* aren't fully in the relationship. Our friend or spouse or partner is unable to connect with us, because our true, valued self is not present. Healthy relationships require us to be healthy.

A tendency to be pessimistic. I know there is debate about the health of a pessimistic perspective. My own personal and professional opinion is that a small dose of the ability to take a pessimistic perspective can be very healthy and beneficial. However, I believe that true pessimism is a symptom of depression, and is unhealthy.

Are you a pessimist? Do you have a fundamentally pessimistic perspective? We can check with those we love and trust, and ask them how they see us. Do they experience us as a pessimist? An optimist? As a realist? Or some combination? We can use their observations to assess ourselves, to check our view of ourself against others' views. And then, ultimately, we have to decide what perspective fits us. And accept that whatever is our dominant, basal perspective, it will have advantages, and disadvantages.

I believe that I'm an optimistic realist; my friends believe I'm a nut. Wait, that's not what I meant to say. I mean, it's true: my friends do think I'm a nut. To this point, though, many of them think I'm overly optimistic, that I see too much good that isn't there, that I see too much hope that is unrealistic. I've thought a lot about that, and I believe my friends' perceptions are probably more accurate than mine. So, I try to be aware of the disadvantages of my cheery perspective, and bring some balance to it. However, I also decided I'm not going to change my realistic optimism, or over-optimism—it helps me to live better, and it took a long time for me to develop it, to get away from being a pessimist, and I sure do like myself more with my optimism. And life is a whole lot more enjoyable. But that's me. You get to decide for yourself who you are, and who you choose to make yourself.

Look for your patterns, so that you can work to bring balance to them when working through difficulties in relationships.

There Are Absolutely No Absolutes
Mostly

Let's go ahead and identify this as ...

Stuhlism #18

There are no absolutes. There are no "should's," no "ought's," "have to's," "must's." There are no "always," no "nevers," no "everyone," no "all of them". None of these global absolutes is accurate. Nor any other absolute.

I know I went on about this earlier. However, this is so important, I wanted to repeat it.

Why harp on this? For several reasons. The first is, this belief empowers an individual. When we have been suffering from emotional hurts and unresolved psychological pain, a consequence can be feelings of powerlessness. The longer we've carried the pain, the stronger the sense of powerlessness. The same is true for the feelings of helplessness and hopelessness. For most of us, we have to see beyond what we know, and empower ourselves. We have to suspend our present beliefs and be ready to adopt or create new ones. And almost always, we need someone's encouragement and support to do what we thought we "shouldn't" do, to feel what we thought we "shouldn't" feel.

A second reason for reiterating this Stuhlism is that wherever the beliefs are, either in our unconscious, subconscious or conscious mind, the beliefs that sustain the painful emotions and dysfunctional thoughts, whatever those beliefs are, changing them is hard (similar to understanding this sentence). As I have already said, we develop beliefs about beliefs, and we attach strong emotions to those beliefs. And the ones that need changing the most? Those are the hardest to change, because they are usually the most deeply buried, and the most intransigent by nature. We think we *need* the belief, that we *have to* have it, hold onto it. It takes real courage, and real tenacity to challenge our beliefs and change.

The third reason for this repetition of no absolutes is to open a person to their truths, and not what they were told was true. As I said just moments ago (if you haven't fallen asleep at the end of the last paragraph), changing is hard. It involves a movement back and forth between uncovering beliefs that are submerged in our mind, to the emotions that sustain them, to the beliefs that sustain *that* emotion or emotions.

It would seem the path is never ending, but it isn't. Remember when I mentioned that when we find what is true for us, we resonate with it? Well, this is where that discovery is so important. As we work through our beliefs and emotions, searching for those that are causing our pain and hurt to remain, we will come upon beliefs and emotions that are as true to us as our name. When we come upon these, either through intentional searches or stumble upon them via the unconscious workings of our psyches, we resonate. I've said this to many of you…and the ones I haven't said it to? Well, I owe you one co-pay back. Nah, just kidding; I'll buy you a donut…As I've said to many, when we find one of our truths it is as if we vibrate, like a tuning fork that's been struck. That's what I mean by resonating with our truths. The sensation is both one of resonance, and of calm, feeling suddenly and strongly grounded, of feeling a balance, of feeling centered. A description that came to me at a time in my life when this occurred was, I heard my inner voice saying, "Oh, man! I've stepped into my own skin!"

Let me give an example before I move on. This may take a minute, so you may grab yourself something to eat. Or do a little blood doping for endurance.

I had a patient once, let's name him Lee (no, it isn't you), who presented with PTSD. He had been a police officer, and had had a great career; had distinguished himself via his work and integrity, and had loved his job. Just loved it.

Tragically, he had to take a disability retirement because he developed PTSD. At first he denied that PTSD was a real thing and didn't believe in therapy (His first statement to me, at our very first meeting: "You know, Dr. John, I don't believe in this counseling bullshit." Yeah, I knew. It made me smile).

Finally, after fighting his symptoms and struggling through several years of anguish as he continued to work, he accepted that he could no longer do his job. He came to realize that he had suffered multiple traumas during his career (Twenty-one, to be exact. He made a list of them, and their intensity and frequency). He knew he had to retire, or he was going to get a colleague hurt or killed, or himself hurt or killed. He changed his beliefs, gradually, about mental illness, about emotional wounds, about healing. Lee saw that emotional wounds are real, and are not a sign of weakness. He discovered that therapy and therapeutic work wasn't bullshit, and could help. He began to deal with each trauma, and as we worked through them, the frequency and intensity of the flashbacks and nightmares greatly diminished.

One trauma remained truly intense though, the most troubling one. He continued to experience powerful flashbacks of it, had actual body memories of it, had sensation experiences (he could *smell* the trauma scene, he could *hear* the voices and sounds and screams, he could *see* the people again).

He continued to work very hard and very directly on this specific trauma; he had come to believe that healing could occur. (I know! A remarkable turn-around. And no, it wasn't me. It was his choice to change. I don't know that I've ever been as impressed by a patient's willingness to change their beliefs and shift their emotions.)

We identified factors that kept the trauma so alive in his life. One was his anger at all his superiors at the trauma scene that day, who did nothing to help, who stood back from the horror of the tragedy because it was too much for them to handle. He realized his anger from that experience kept the trauma alive. So we developed some exercises where he could understand those supervisors differently, where he could accept what they were unable to do, and where he could (miraculously) forgive them for their failures. And with that, a great deal of his anger dissipated.

And yet, the trauma was still with him. He continued to have some nightmares of this specific trauma, though with much less frequency, and much reduced intensity. Finally, after one such night, Lee sat down in our next session and asked me, "What the fuck, Doc!? Why the fuck is this bullshit trauma hanging around? It is royally fucking with me, and I'm about god damned over it!" (Yes, he was *exquisite* at prayer language.)

I suggested that there was something else holding the trauma in place, and so we went searching. And we found it…and this is the reason I share this story. The second factor that locked the trauma was a surprise and shock to both of us. As we worked back through the trauma again, looking for the key that would unlock its grip on my friend and set him free at last, we identified a very specific, powerful component. During the trauma, a mother was in anguish over the suicide of her young son, and she was keening in grief… as my friend said, it's a sound that a person will never forget once they've heard it, and an emotional state that might kill the person if it is not interrupted, if the mother couldn't be brought out of her state of abject, absolute despair.

So, my friend (and, yes, I refer to all of you, all of my patients, as friends. I think of you that way. I'll explain why towards the end of the book)…my friend held the mother, and blocked her view of the gruesome scene of her son's horrific suicide. My friend comforted her, and helped that mother back from the edge of despair.

Lee said, "I had to get her to stop keening, to break her intense despair. She absolutely couldn't go on like that—it would have destroyed her." And with that, two hypotheses came to my mind, so I shared them. With the first hypothesis, I said, "You know, it may be that your mind keeps recalling this flashback to you, so that you can see and feel pride at what you did for her."

"But that wouldn't be right!" he said. "I was just doing my job."

"It's okay to feel pride. You can be 'just doing your job,' and still feel great pride in what you did," I offered.

That belief struck him; he hadn't realized that he held the belief that if he felt pride, he was somehow being arrogant, being haughty. Lee thought he would be violating something his parents taught him, both in words and in the way they lived their lives: that pride was a "bad" emotion. That pride was the opposite of humility (note: it is not). That if you felt proud of yourself, you were elevating yourself above others.

Lee realized that he struggled to shift his belief about pride because of another belief, that he would be offending and betraying his parents, whom he loved and admired.

I suggested a belief I had discovered for myself, that there is a certain point in our life where we realize that we know better than our parents did. That we supersede our parents. And that this is not betraying them or diminishing their importance or dishonoring them; that this superseding of our parents is a powerful, positive, healthy transition in life.

"Why is that?" he asked.

"Because, and this is only what I believe—it doesn't have to be your truth—because at some point, we discover that we know better for our life than our parents can. No matter how good and brilliant and wise parents are, they can never know our life better than we can, because we are the one who lives our life, and who knows and discovers what is true for ourself," I offered. "And, this isn't dishonoring at all; it is something that every person goes through, either intentionally or unconsciously. Every person. Your parents went through this transition with their parents, and their parents before them. It is actually honoring your parents, who raised you to be yourself and to discover and be who you are."

That was a shock to Lee. And it opened a gateway for him to find almost complete healing from that trauma. Almost. But there was one factor still lingering.

He kept hearing the mother's keening. He couldn't stop hearing it. He believed with all his heart that he had done the right thing to help that mother to come back from the brink of despair. And he had. He had acted in the very best interests of that mother, with true love and compassion and professionalism.

And that's when I had the second insight, and so shared my second hypothesis: that he had not only pulled that mother back from the total emotional destruction for the mother's benefit, but also *because he couldn't stand the keening either. That he had to make it stop for himself as well.*

"Well, that would make me a total, selfish douche bag," he said. (Reminder: Lee was artistic with prayers.)

"No—it would make you normal. The two aren't mutually exclusive—your acting for the best benefit of that mother, and for a benefit of your own. That happens to us, and it doesn't make you a bad person, or a selfish person. It makes you normal. It is okay."

And it was that belief change that freed my patient. Once he realized the negative, selfcritical beliefs that sustained the trauma, and the fear of what he would be if he accepted a new belief, he was freed. Lee found full healing of that trauma.

Here are the most significant points about this amazing patient. The beliefs he had to change were *fundamentally healthy beliefs, held with the best of intentions.* By recognizing his pride in himself, he wasn't betraying or being disloyal to his parents. By accepting that in his choices during the traumatic event, he was receiving a benefit as well, he was exercising care for himself as well as for the grieving mother. Unconsciously, he had felt guilt that he was glad he could get the mother to stop wailing, to come back from emotional destruction; that he was glad for himself as well as the mother. Lee unconsciously thought that he was being selfish, and so had, again unconsciously, grouped himself with all his supervisors who that day had not done their jobs because "they were taking care of themselves."

I was so appreciative to sit with and work with this man. I was so grateful that I could find perspectives that helped find healing. Oh, trust me—I've shortened this story...I haven't shared all the inaccurate hypotheses I offered; I haven't shared with you all the rabbit holes I unwittingly took us down. There was nothing miraculous about me in my work with him. In other words, yes, I helped with his healing, and I'm proud to do so, but the miracle was his courage to face what was so hard, and make the changes that seemed so wrong about his beliefs that were actually right and true. That's where the wonder is; that is where it is appropriate to hold and share honor—with his courage and tenacity, his strength to change and heal.

Wow, that was long! And the illustration has revealed several other guiding beliefs I hold, so let's move on and see if I can get them revealed. "Maybe in an abbreviated manner, Dr. J?!" Yes, I agree. I'll work to be brief.

You Just Made Those Up

You are correct.

What you are about to get, I've made up.

As you know, I like creating. Not only do I find it meaningful and fulfilling, I find a lot of creating serves another purpose—to be of better effect for you, for others.

Here are two words I've created, why I created them, and how you might find them helpful.

d'BLARD

Originally, when I first constructed this word, it was BLARD. Just BLARD. As I said it our loud, I thought to myself, "Oh, my….That is way too back-woods, up-in-the-hollers East Tennessee." BLARD didn't have enough cache, at least for me.

So, I made it French. I love France—the wine, the cheeses, the breads, the desserts. Whoa! Maybe I just love French food. But I love the language also, and because spoken French sounds so classy, so sophisticated, I went across the Atlantic with my word, and it became d'BLARD. As you've probably guessed, or already knew, it is an acronym. And it stands for:

deep **B**reathe

Let go

Accept

Relax

Detach

These are the skills that I find help us to break anxious cycles and to bring us into the present. When we use these skills, we reduce stress, anxiety, fear, anger—all of the arousing emotions. For me, they are the skills that help us to live more mindfully.

My editor, bless her heart (and we all know what that means in church circles), asks "What's the difference between 'letting go' and 'detaching'." Funny; none of *you* ever needed that clarification. But, once more, I aim to please. Letting go, for me, is a cognitive exercise; it is changing the thoughts we hold about wanting to make a change in something external to us. It is changing our belief from wanting and working to making something different that is not in our control, to releasing our need to change that external aspect. Detachment is much more of an emotional exercise; it is disengaging our emotions from a situation. Let's see if an example helps.

Let's say I have a difficulty with a cousin, with whom I once had a great friendship. We'll say her name is Lucretia. As we grew up, we were really close; we had fun together, we double dated while in high school, we went to the same church youth group and learned and shared the same beliefs that we were taught, that all people are equal, that every person deserves love and honor and respect, regardless of their race or religion or orientation, and that every person is a child of god and is loved and valued equally. No one is above others.

Over time, Lucretia began to change; she started to embrace racist beliefs, she began to fly a confederate flag at her house, she campaigned for laws to outlaw interracial marriages and she supported, financially and as a volunteer, a group who wanted to make slavery legal once more.

Lucretia's changes distressed me emotionally. Here was someone I loved, liked, admired, was emotionally close to and whose friendship I had always cherished, and she had become someone who believed, espoused and actively worked towards goals that I found not only different from mine, but appalling and reprehensible. And not only did Lucretia change herself, she began to push me to change to believe like her. She would get overbearing with her beliefs, she would argue and berate me for what I believed. She would not only tell me I was wrong, she would be very critical and judgmental of me, she would try to belittle me at family gatherings, she would call me names and be sarcastic and hostile to me whenever we were together (which became less and less frequent. Uh, duh).

The coup de grace came when Lucretia asked me to give her $50,000 as a contribution for her campaign to abolish the 13th Amendment. When I said "No," Lucretia became really angry with me, told me I was rich, and that I "owed her" because she was family, that "family always came first," that "you never turned your back on your family," that "blood was thicker than water," and that whatever I had I should share because I was her cousin and she had the right to ask it of me and I had the absolute responsibility to fulfill whatever she asked.

Of course, initially I was an emotional wreck because of this. I was hurt. I was shocked. I felt distressed and sad, angry and dismayed. I felt disbelief at Lucretia's changes, and betrayal at the way she had moved so far away from the values and beliefs that we had grown up with. I felt torn— was I supposed to help her, simply because she was family? Was I to violate my own beliefs and ethics? Did I "owe" her, because of the true love, closeness and friendship we had for so long?

And, I wanted to see a change. I wanted to see Lucretia change; I wanted her to return to the beliefs and actions that we were raised with. I wanted my loving, caring, kind, thoughtful cousin back, the person who was once one of my best friends.

I was a wreck—I know, many people believe that I truly am a wreck. That's a different issue. I was emotionally distraught. And I was behaviorally overwhelmed, because not only did I want to refuse support to Lucretia, I wanted to actively work against her efforts for what I believed was truly evil. My work suffered, my relationships suffered, my sleep was disturbed and nothing tasted good, which was the worst symptom of all for my inner child who is a little fat boy.

I knew I had to do something, or I'd experience drastic consequences like losing my job or destroying my marriage or getting a Tennessee waterfall haircut, a.k.a. a mullet. Then I thought, "Hey, what do I recommend to patients? I suggest they d'BLARD." So, that's what I began to do.

I began to do some deep Breathing.

I started to Let Go (reason for this example)—I gave up the idea of Lucretia changing *for me to feel better*. I didn't need Lucretia to do anything different for me to be okay.

I Accepted...this was the situation as it is, and I could neither change the externals, nor did I need to for me to create peace and balance and calm within myself.

I Relaxed. I intentionally chose to relax my body, which helped to relax my mind.

I Detached (the other reason for this example)—I disengaged my emotions. How, you ask? Great question. I decided that my emotions were my responsibility. I chose healthy beliefs—that I don't 'have to do what Lucretia says; that I choose what I believe about family, that I decide if my choices and beliefs are true for me, not someone else; that I can be okay and even fulfilled without any one person in my life, that I don't "need" Lucretia's love, support, respect, etc. There is nothing I need from Lucretia for me to be okay. I chose the belief that Lucretia's opinions and feelings *have nothing to do with me!, say nothing about me!, and mean nothing about me!* Just like Mrs. Drummel before.

I hope this example helps, and makes clear what I see as the difference between letting go and detachment. Guess my editor will tell me soon enough.

My second creation is also an acronym.

C'PADH. It's clearly not French. Possibly Indian? Maybe Gaelic? Honestly, I'm not sure. I just couldn't find a better way to arrange the letters that I needed to use. So,

C'PADH it became—if anyone knows a language it aligns with, please share with me.

C'PADH. It stands for:

Consistent

Persistent

Assertive

Direct

Honest

I use this acronym to help me remember the fundamental tenets of the most effective communication, most of the time. Let me offer some expansion.

So often, we get caught up in trying to make things perfect: the perfect date, the perfect sandwich (as if every sandwich isn't already perfect), the perfect birthday party, the perfect set of teeth. Our society is obsessed with perfection, which is pretty stupid, in my opinion. ("Dr. J, that sounds pretty critical and judgmental, don't ya' think?" And my response is, "It's not critical or judgmental if it's true.") Why pursue perfection? Well, I mean, other than in sporting events. And maybe orchestras. Certainly we want perfection for rocket launching of astronauts.

Okay! Maybe some forms of perfection seeking are good. What I'm referring to is perfection within ourselves and with our interactions with others. Here, there is no perfection.

So, to get away from an impossible and unnecessary goal, the first two skills are offered.

If our goal isn't perfection, what can it be? My belief: our goal is to be consistent and persistent. These are attainable goals, they are reasonable and realistic, and they greatly help communication.

Of course, I hold the assumption that we are working to make ourselves and our communications more and more effective. It wouldn't do anyone any good if I was consistently and persistently an annoying butt-munch. But if we want to build healthy relationships, and we work to see those relationships get stronger and more satisfying, we will need to be consistent and persistent.

Practicing these two skills also gets us away from the "one experience evaluation." That is where we have a difficult interaction with someone and we judge the relationship by that single experience. "Consistent" helps us to be reliable over time; "persistent" helps to extend ourselves over time. Both help us to think of our relationships over extended interactions, rather than a single experience.

Assertive. Direct. Honest. These skills are specifically about how we speak and talk with others. Now, some caveats. This does not mean we *always* have to be assertive and direct and honest. There are four forms language takes, and we all know them: passive, passive-aggressive, assertive, and aggressive. (I recently heard of a fifth form: aggressive-aggressive. I think I'd like to develop that skill.) And each form has its place; each form can be used, and in a healthy manner.

But if we want the clearest, most open communication, we work to be assertive, direct and honest.

I won't go on about these skills of communication, because that could be a whole second book. I'll leave it to say that as we work to practice these five skills, and we work to enhance and develop them, we will become so much more effective, healthy and influential in our relationships. And with ourselves.

Why Keep Asking Why?

And nooooo, "Why not?" is not an answer. Answering a question with a question is not only maddening, it is rude and frustrating and an obfuscation of real communication. Answering a question with a question is manipulative and evasive and is not intended for real understanding, but for arguing and hiding and trying to win an argument. It's a horrible practice, and nooo, that's not a criticism or a judgement, because once again, it's true. Well, my truth.

Phew. I guess I needed to get that off my chest.

As I was making my way through my doctoral program, I had many professors who taught that you should never ask a patient "why?".

"Why not?" I asked. Which seemed to piss them off, but that was their issue. After all, they had already cussed, i.e. used a "should." When they got over their snit, they explained that asking a patient why put the patient on the spot.

What the hell?! A patient is on the spot already; they've come to therapy because they need help, they want help in order to heal, though most patients can't quite word it that way.

Most patients say something like "I'm miserable," or "I'm depressed," or "I'm all fucked up, and I've totally fucked my life."

Asking why is a gift. With all due respect to my professors, most for whom I hold great respect, there's been a tendency in psychology to see patients as extremely fragile, and therefore to be treated with extreme gentleness. What I believe is that most patients, though they are suffering and may feel fragile, are amazingly strong and resilient; after all, whatever emotional wounds or psychological pains they are suffering, the patient has been carrying them for a long time. That takes real strength. Not to mention the strength it takes to ask for help—it is the strongest person who can admit he or she is weak and needs help.

So, I've always asked "why" of patients. I know, you know. I've asked it of you a thousand times. And I suggest that patients ask it of themselves.

The beauty of why is it sends us exploring. Remember above, when I said healing is the task of tracking pain? Well, following the "why" is one way of tracking. Get ready, because I'm going to give an example.

A patient, let's call him Edgar, tells me, "My partner accused me of no longer caring about him. That was so offensive; it hurt so bad."

And I responded, "Edgar, this may sound like a stupid question, but why?"

"Why what, Dr. J.?"

"Why did it hurt so bad?"

"Well, because... because we've been together for so long, I guess. Because he shouldn't be cruel. I'm not sure why."

"Was your partner being cruel when he said it?"

"No, Jamie's never been cruel."

"Then why did it hurt?"

"I'm not sure... maybe because I feel like he doesn't recognize all the things I do for him. Maybe because he seems indifferent to the ways I give him love."

"Have you ever told Jamie this? That you feel he doesn't realize all you do for him?"

"No, of course not... that would be cruel?"

"Would it though? Why would it be cruel to share that you feel there's distance between you? It's just expressing that you're missing Jamie, emotionally. It seems that Jamie's feeling the same way."

"Maybe I'm afraid of what the answer will be?"

"Edgar, if Jamie is expressing the same thing you've been feeling, a sadness...the sense that you two have grown apart, maybe he's missing you too. Maybe your fear can be soothed, if you believe Jamie wants the same thing you do, to be close again."

"Maybe...maybe..."

We'll leave Edgar there, wondering what the hell his psychologist is thinking.

Asking "why" encourages us to explore our mind and our heart. And we will usually have to explore much further than we anticipate, because our first several answers to "why" we already know. They are what we're already aware of. It is into the unknown that we have to go, and why can lead us there.

I have several guidelines for asking why.

The first is, be gentle when asking why. I am gentle when I ask patients, and patients should be gentle when asking others and asking themselves. So often the difficulty of asking "why" is not the question, it is the way it is asked. All too often, "why" sounds like an accusation, like a judgement waiting to happen. If we can ask it out of real curiosity and concern, then "why" becomes an invitation.

The second guideline is to keep asking why. We have to get past our known answers, the beliefs and feelings we are already aware of, and get to the ones we are not aware of. This takes tenacity, a willingness to dig for what is hidden. It is hard, but I find that the result is almost always healing, a liberation. And new or renewed life.

Multiple patients have asked me, "But where do you stop? The 'why's' could go on forever." To which I offer my third guideline. Keep asking 'why', and find your answers. And then ask "Is that all?" Our minds have a wisdom all their own, is what I've come to discover and what I believe. When we are searching for our answers, for healing and emotional resolution, our mind will continue to tell us, "There's more there…. There's something more… there is still a thought or feeling that is needing to be uncovered, addressed. Keep going." Or, our mind will tell us, "That's enough for now; we've found what we need for now. There may be more later, but for now, this is enough."

So, why ask why?

Because.

Hahahaha—I made another joke! I was funny!

Well, maybe not. "Because" is as annoying and maddening as "Why not?" as an answer. The real answer is…

Asking why guides us in healing. So ask it, over and over again, and follow the answers that emerge within you.

This Chapter Sounds Depressing

Maybe that's because it's about depression. But, if I write this well, by the end you'll feel hopeful. Which is reasonable, because there is hope for depression.

Let's begin with some definitions, because depression isn't simply a single experience or entity.

There is a classic definition; depression is anger turned inwards. When we are depressed, we are really very angry and have suppressed it.

A second definition of depression is that it is a biological illness, that it is a disorder in the organ of the brain, where the brain functions at below normal, healthy levels, and this is caused by genetics or a failure of the brain system. This kind of depression will almost always require medication to manage, just as diabetes will require insulin and hypertension will require blood pressure medication.

The third definition of depression is that it is a psychological disorder, that the brain and mind are disordered via some experience or trauma a person has endured but that hasn't yet been resolved. This kind of depression will almost certainly require some form of therapy to heal, whether with a trained professional or by one's own intentional efforts.

The fourth definition comes from Scott Peck, the author of *The Road Less Traveled, People of the Lie,* and several other books. Dr. Peck writes that depression is actually grief work over a decision that has been made but not yet admitted into awareness. Fascinating, and from personal experience, I know this definition is accurate and true.

A fifth definition, which is actually one I postulate, is that depression isn't an emotion itself, but merely a cognitive construct to mask much more painful emotions of despair and anguish, shame and guilt, grief and hopelessness.

Five definitions, and all of them are accurate. Damn, how do we figure it out at all? Well, there are ways. I believe that these definitions are not mutually exclusive, and actually the experience of depression can be several of these descriptors at once. Here are my guiding beliefs about depression.

First, there are people who are born with a biological depression, just as there are people who are born with near-sightedness. The organ of their brain has a slight dysfunction and the neurotransmitters work below optimal levels. This kind of depression requires medication to truly treat it, though therapy can greatly help in healing.

Second, even if our depression is of the psychological nature, when we are depressed, we are depressed at the

118

cellular level; our neurons are functioning at below normal levels. This means that there are times when, even though the depression is due to some form of emotional or psychological hurt, medication may be necessary to help put the depression in remission, to help our neurons to work within the normal, healthy range. In these instances, therapy alone can't heal the depression, and medication is needed. For some people, after they have resolved the emotional wound, they are able to go off their medications and return to their normal, happy selves. For others, the shift in the brain chemistry is such that medication will remain a requirement for the depression to be in remission.

Third, we in psychology say that medication stabilizes, and therapy heals. Why? Because it makes us feel better and sound much more important. Well, there's that, but also because even when the brain is functioning within normal levels, we have to resolve the cognitions and emotions that are causing distress. And, even when someone's depression is of the biological kind, the brain develops habits in the ways of thoughts and patterns. These thought habits can be dysfunctional and unhealthy, and so require change, which requires therapy.

Fourth, it is my belief that it is essential to reorder the way we think about and talk about depression. So often, we say "Damn, I'm depressed." I believe that this is harmful to us, because it doesn't give enough distance between us and the illness.

Think of it this way—we don't say, "Damn, I'm cancer." Well, at least not if we're of sound mind and spirit. We say, "Damn, I have cancer." There is a degree of separation there, and that separation is helpful for healing. So too with mental illnesses. Because we associate ourselves so much with our thoughts and emotions, when we speak of mental illnesses it is even more important to distinguish the illness we're suffering from who we really are, from our truer selves.

For me, words are important, and the way we shape our words can shape us. This is why I encourage small shifts in our self-expressions. Not "I'm depressed," rather "I have depression." Not "I'm bi-polar" but "I have the illness of bi-polar disorder." Not "I'm a basket case," rather… well, maybe we'll let this descriptor stand.

There is another reason, for me, to change our language. When we gain this degree of separation, we are able to see the symptoms of depression for what they are, symptoms of an illness, *not* a weakness on our part in our choices. When I'm suffering depression, the illness generates symptoms: just like if I catch the flu, I suffer symptoms of weakness, fever, chills, sweating, possibly nausea and a loss of appetite (the worst!, says my inner child, who is still that little fat boy standing at the kitchen counter, licking his lips as he stares at the cookies and asks, "Can I have one? Or five?"). When I suffer depression, my low mood is a symptom, it is not me being weak-minded; my pessimistic outlook is a symptom, it is not me being a pessimist; my lethargy is a symptom, it is not being lazy or unmotivated.

What is essential about this, you ask? Great question.

When I see depression as an illness and the dysfunctional, negative and critical thoughts and emotions as symptoms of that illness, I *stop judging myself!* Which is a crucial step in beginning to effect our depression. We're not fighting our "failure." We're fighting our illness, and learning to manage our illness.

And one of the most important steps in healing is *to stop judging ourselves!* Remember how I said negative thoughts sustain painful emotions? Well, there's not much more negative than judging ourselves. And we are good at it; we bad-person ourselves nearly to death. Tragically, sometimes to death. When we learn how to accept ourselves, and describe ourselves without judgment, criticism and negative talk, we take leaps forward in healing.

There are some who believe that if we don't judge ourselves, then we are giving ourselves excuses for our choices and behaviors. I don't agree with this view (uh, duh); I believe we can learn to describe ourselves accurately, with stark honesty and candor, and hold ourselves accountable, without self-criticism. After all, most mental illnesses are overflowing with negative self-talk and self-criticism; negative self-talk and self-criticism are symptoms of almost every mental illness. To reduce them, and try to catch our negative thoughts and adjust them, is a great step in healing.

Oh, and since we're on the subject of depression, here's another Stuhlism.

Stuhlism #19

In almost all instances, when someone succumbs to suicide, it is best understood as the mental illness overcoming the body.

Just as there are times when the illness of cancer overcomes the body's ability to fight off the illness, and the body succumbs, and the person dies, so to with the mental illness of which suicide is the symptom. We don't say, "Well, she killed herself by cancer," neither should we say "Well, he killed himself by suicide." More accurately, and surely more caring and sensitive to any loved ones grieving the death, I think it most helpful to say "It's tragic; her illness of depression overcame her."

My hope and goal, when I work with folks with depression, is not to necessarily immediately heal the depression—that is always a long term goal, but not something that can be done in a minute. Rather, what I hope is that a person can learn to *effect* their depression, that, through shifts in their perspective, changing of beliefs, and soothing and understanding of the accompanying emotions, they can reduce the intensity and severity of the symptoms, just a single iota (remember the iota!). If a person can do that, then they gain some power in relation to their depression, which generates hope and empowerment and motivation to continue the path of healing and wellness.

Did I promise a story of my own dealings with depression? I didn't? Oh, shoot—well, then, you don't have to read the following.

In 1984, I had several very difficult experiences, and I found myself questioning my vocation, and what I wanted to do with my professional life (at the time, I was the minister of a church). And so, thankfully, at that time the Presbyterian Church had a Vocational Reassessment Center in Decatur, Georgia, with programs designed for just such confused souls as me. And so I entered one of their programs and throughout that year, I did a lot of reading, writing (and arithmetic!), journaling and therapy. I also took a battery of vocational assessment instruments and some psychological and personality profiles (I failed my personality tests. Apparently, I have no personality). I then spent four days at the Assessment Center.

It was during these four days that I realized that I had been depressed the past year, and shared this with my therapist there, a Dr. Bob Urie—wonderful man, and a real gift to me. He turned to his bookshelf, pulled out a book and said, "John, Scott Peck writes that depression is really grief work over an unconscious decision that's been made but not yet admitted into awareness."

And I said, "Well, shit." Because in that moment, my depression lifted. Gone. It was literally gone, just like that, because I knew what decision my unconscious had made (my unconscious mind is a whole lot wiser than my conscious mind). I knew in that moment I was leaving the ministry. I knew I wanted to; I knew I wanted to become a psychologist, and my grief work? I had been grieving all those unconscious hopes and dreams I'd had for ministry, all those projections of how my future would be. And I was totally at peace with giving up all those beliefs, because I knew in my heart I wanted to become a psychologist and a therapist. Which is

124

exactly what happened, though it took several years (ten to be exact) to arrive at my goal.

It is a decision I have never regretted. It is a decision that I have thanked my unconscious for countless times. It is probably the truest part of me, being a psychologist and therapist, and the past twenty seven years have been a delight—but I've already told you that.

The real point to this story? That the definition of depression as grief work over an unconscious decision made but not admitted into awareness, is real. I know that definition to be true, because I experienced it.

This may not be true for you, and that's okay. It is true for me, and that's enough. The power of this story is that in finding the correct definition, the accurate naming of what I was experiencing, was liberating. I was freed from depression, and freed to my future.

This Chapter Makes Me Nervous

Anxiety. Also known as Fear. As Stress. As Worry. As Lady Jessica Atreides said in the recent movie Dune: "Fear is the mind killer. Fear is the little death that brings obliteration. I will face my fear, and I will permit it to pass over me and through me."

I believe this. I also know that we can't completely eliminate anxiety from our lives. Anxiety is hard wired into us, as a survival mechanism from eons ago when life was truly eat or be eaten, kill or be killed. It is the fight-flight-freeze mechanism. So, it is impossible to live a completely anxiety-free life.

The challenge is to effect anxiety, to lower its intensity and duration (here's that iota thing again). And to build emotional resilience and detachment, so that we react to fewer and fewer external stimuli.

Of course, this isn't easy, especially as our anxiety escalates. As our level of anxiety rises, our mind tends to produce fewer and fewer options, and feel more and more trapped.

How do we break this cycle? How do we deal with the mind killer? There are steps. And there is information that is useful to build our strength in coping, and to apply when we are beset with anxiety.

The first bit of information is that when we get anxious in our mind, in our thoughts, our body gets tense. The more anxious our thoughts, the more tense our body. The opposite is true also; if our body is tense, our mind will be anxious. The good news is that when our body is calm, our mind is calm, and when our mind is calm, then our body is calm. The mind and the body, with regards to anxiety, can't be in opposition.

With this knowledge, we can effect anxiety in two ways. If we lower the tension in our body/calm our body, the intensity of our anxious thoughts will reduce. And, if we calm our mind by choosing healthy beliefs and positive thoughts, our body will calm. We can reach and effect anxiety via either direction, mind or body.

Let me give an example of how our thoughts can powerfully effect our anxiety. I once saw a young man, let's call him Brutus, who came to me because of some fairly crippling anxiety. Brutus was 11 years old, and while on vacation, his family was in a frightening near accident on the interstate. It was night, a car passed them, then blew a tire and began to swerve erratically in front of them. Brutus's mother slammed on the breaks and was able to avoid hitting the other car, but the car Brutus was in spun around several times and ended up in the medium, facing traffic.

The good news was, no one was hurt. The family car didn't even suffer damage. The bad news was that from that point on, Brutus was terrified to get in a car, literally terrified. He would travel in cars, but he would have anxiety attacks and panic attacks, it would take him upwards of an hour to get in a car, and he would arrive at his destination drenched in sweat and mentally exhausted. Because of the profuse sweating, I didn't allow Brutus to sit in my leather chair, 'cause, you know, gross.... Of course, I just made that up, and it isn't true.

So, Brutus' parents brought him to therapy. Brutus had readily agreed to therapy, though he wasn't sure what good it would do. First, I invited Brutus to share what happened— sometimes, just telling a traumatic story can have a beneficial effect. Next, we named what Brutus was suffering: anxiety attacks, panic attacks, and dread. Putting the accurate names on the emotions Brutus was feeling brought him another bit of relief (Btw, the way we determined the accurate names? Brutus and I went through lists of emotions, and Brutus chose what fit with what he was feeling). Then, Brutus and I worked to normalize his reactions: that high fear and anxiety and caution were absolutely understandable in this situation—this gave Brutus another bit of relief. We also removed all judgements from the emotions; Brutus came to accept his feelings for what they were, and didn't judge them as bad or weak or pathetic. Once again, some relief.

And yet, the anxiety persisted. It was less intense, but it was still there. That's when an idea dropped into my head from I-don't-know-where. I said, "Hey, Brutus. Let's do some math." Brutus liked math. So, here's what we did: we made an estimate of how many cars passed by Brutus' car on the road in a day. We calculated it was 287 cars a day (it was either we were very specific in our calculations, or we made the damn number up—I can't remember which. But it was a number Brutus accepted; that's key.) Then, we said, "Okay, there are 365 days in a year. So, we'll multiple 287 by that," and we got 104,755. Brutus then said, "I've been alive 11 years, so let's multiple 104,755 by 11," and we got 1,152,305.

At this point I said, "Brutus, in your eleven years of life, you've had 1,152,305 chances to have an accident, and you've had one. "Hmmm," Brutus answered, then he added, "Wait, Dr. J. There have been two leap years, so we have to add <quick calculations> 574 to that last number." So, we made that addition, and came up with 1,152,879 instances where a car passed by the car Brutus rode in.

"So, my odds are...1 in 1,152,879...for an accident." Brutus smiled at me, and said, "You know, I can live with those odds."

And he did; his intense anxiety was dismissed and Brutus was able to ride in cars again without his punishing stress and anxiety attacks and panic attacks. In fact, without dread or fear.

I was impressed by Brutus's shift; actually, I was amazed. I was also reminded that *when we change a belief, we can change our perceptions and dismiss or heal an emotion.* Does this happen all the time? Sadly, no; at least, not this dramatically and this suddenly. But it can happen; it does happen. The hard work is finding the beliefs that sustain the painful emotions.

One last thought before I move on from anxiety. As we begin our healing, it is essential that we accurately name what we are experiencing. And I find that with anxiety, all too often the person isn't really *anxious*, they are actually feeling *anger or agitation or annoyance*. What a change this makes to the therapeutic work of healing, to correctly identify what needs resolution. Without this correct identification, it's like trying to fix a car's alignment by working on the exhaust system.

If we get stuck in therapy, it is often a good choice to look closely on what we believe the problem is, and make sure we have it accurately identified.

The Beautiful Self-Valuing Feeling

Anger.

Yes, anger is beautiful. Not necessarily in the expression of it—that can get very ugly very fast and end up with fights and road rage, murders and war, toddler tantrums and eviscerating evangelists. What is beautiful about anger is the *emotion* of it. Anger as a *feeling* is beautiful, because anger is a self-valuing feeling.

Let me explain. I've gone through this description with all of you, I believe, but here it is, in print.

Anger is evoked in a person when they experience one of three experiences, or any combination of them: rejection, injustice/unfairness, or oppression. Some folks would add "offense" as an experience that evokes anger, but I happen to think that "offense" is captured by the first three. And, since this is my schema, and I've been sharing it this way for decades, I'm just gonna go with the three experiences. If you'd feel better adding "offense," please do so.

When we experience rejection, injustice/unfairness, oppression or a combination of them, anger emerges. Why is that? Because it is our inner self saying, "Hey, I deserve reasonable acceptance. I have enough worth to be treated fairly and justly. I have enough value to be respected and not put down or held down."

Our inner self knows worth and value; sadly, we lose touch with this deep true nature of ourselves as we grow. Ah, my editor, god love her, wonders if cultural conditioning is the reason for losing touch with our deep sense of true value and worth. The answer, of course, is yes. And, the loss is also a natural aspect of growth and maturity. We are social creatures; as we grow and develop, we innately measure ourselves against others. We see that Betty Lou reads faster than us, we watch Louis run past us on the playground, we find we ate six pieces of pizza when the rest of our classmates ate only three. And this doesn't even account for all the challenges of mind and thoughts and learning. Anxiety, feelings of insecurity, inadequacy, inferiority emerge naturally (and they have useful, healthy purposes). No one escapes these feelings. A person could be raised in a perfect environment and culture and the feelings of doubt and insecurity and inferiority would still arise. Those feelings are inescapable. Which is both okay, understandable and acceptable. The issue is how to respond to them.

No matter how intense and extreme the feelings of insecurity and its accompanying bullies, no matter how pervasive and dominant these painful feelings seem to be, they are never able to destroy the life enhancing feelings of worth and value and beauty. The sense of esteem, worth and value are still there; they are in us always. And because anger is a self-valuing feeling, when we experience anger, we are having an experience of worth and value. This is why anger is a beautiful emotion.

Of course, no one (well, maybe no one who is mentally healthy) wants to *live* angry, to *be* an angry person. To feel anger is healthy; to resolve anger, and learn to reduce our sensitivity to experiences that evoke anger, is healthier. Just like with all the other emotions, the goal of dealing with anger is not to ever feel anger again. The goal is build our resilience, our detachment and our solid sense of self-acceptance to such a point that we get angry at fewer and fewer things, and we resolve our anger more and more quickly.

Whenever we feel anger, we also feel hurt; the two feelings are always partners. Often, when we're aware of feeling hurt, we are not aware of the feelings of anger; the opposite is true as well, that when we feel anger, we are often unaware of feeling hurt. The significance of this is that to truly, fully heal from an experience that evoked anger, we must realize our feelings of hurt and resolve them as well.

Managing anger is a skill set that includes: identify the anger; clarify the anger; vent the anger; develop a plan (which, by the way, is not "where do I hide the body?"), and look forward and not back, because anger tends to keep us looking into the past.

Those skills are for managing anger, but they don't resolve anger. The resolution of anger is done via three tasks. These are tasks, because we almost never do them a single time; we must do them over and over again, with deeper understanding and effect each iteration.

The three tasks for anger resolution are: understanding, acceptance and forgiveness.

A word about these three. Understanding means that we look at whatever experience evoked our anger and build new perspectives on it. We learn to observe by shifting our perspective so that we can see the experience from another's point of view, or several different points of view. And, much like an excellent story (say, the parables in the gospels), each time we look back and try to understand the experience, we are able to see differently, see with more depth and recognize the complexities that went into the experience.

Acceptance is not approval. Acceptance is simply the acknowledgement that the experience happened, and that we don't have to have the experience removed from our life for us to be okay.

Forgiveness is often the most difficult of these tasks. It is important to recognize what forgiveness *isn't*.

Forgiveness is *not* forgetting. We forgive, and we remember.

Forgiveness is *not* minimizing. We are honest about the size and significance of the anger-evoking experience.

Forgiveness is *not* saying we can return to the same relationship. We forgive, and require the relationship to change. We may even forgive and end the relationship.

Forgiveness is *not* saying there are no consequences. We can forgive and work to enact consequences.

What, then, is forgiveness? Forgiveness is the setting down of our anger, the letting go of our anger, because we have come to know that we no longer need our anger to remain safe in relation to the other person/experience.

Forgiveness, then, is for the forgiver. Forgiveness sets us free, because (and this is significant enough for it to be bolded, as a Stuhlism)…

Stuhlism #20

Anger is a very strong bond. Whomever we are angry at, our anger keeps that person or persons tied tightly into our life.

I like to describe the bonds of anger this way. When we are angry at someone, who, let's say, has been a real sack of shit to us, then our anger is like taking that sack of shit and throwing it across our shoulder and carrying it around on our back. In August. At three p.m.. In the bright sunlight, heat, and humidity. A very unpleasant image, right? Which is just what unresolved anger is.

Another description of the bonds of anger: anger is like putting a fishing hook in my mouth, and handing the other person the fishing pole. All that happens is that I get yanked around, over and over again. Again, a very unpleasant image.

There are other descriptions besides the two I made up, which are equally helpful: anger is giving another person space in my mind rent free; anger is a shut door that traps us in a room of red; anger is wasted energy, a waste of our life force. Possibly, you have a description of anger that is particularly meaningful to you; if so, excellent. Keep it. If not, it can be very helpful to healthy living to find a description of anger that you resonate with.

Understanding. Acceptance. Forgiveness. These are the three tasks that resolve anger. And yes, we usually have to do them multiple times. Which is perfectly okay. There is no failure if we find ourselves returning to an experience that hurt or angered us. We continue to work through our understanding, our acceptance and our forgiveness and become more and more free of the feelings of anger and hurt. I like to call this an ascending cycle of affirmation: we realize that though we were rejected and treated unjustly, we are okay. Because we are okay, we can look at the experience and see it with a new perspective. When we understand more, we are able to accept more. And as we exercise these skills, we find ourselves more and more free and whole and healthy; we realize…we are okay. We are good.

You know I love examples, and here's one from early on in my career.

Decades ago, a young woman…we'll call her Gertie, short for Gertrude…came to her first appointment and stated, "Dr. John. I need help with my anger, because my life is being consumed with rage and hatred."

Here are the circumstances of Gertie's life and anger. Several years before seeing me, Gertie's brother had been murdered. He was killed in a drug deal gone bad (he was buying drugs because he suffered the illness of addiction). The two men who killed her brother had both been caught, tried, convicted and were serving very long jail terms.

What had Gertie trapped was that every year or two, the two men would have parole hearings, and Gertie would go speak against their parole. And it was this continued freely selfchosen responsibility that kept Gertie's anger and hatred and rage (they are all on the anger continuum) inflamed in her.

We began therapy specifically for her anger, and I shared the little schema above with her. Gertie was an amazing patient: she took the structure, and applied it to her circumstance with remarkable courage and integrity. We met for six sessions. I barely had to talk (I know. None of you can believe that could happen); Gertie would come to a session and walk through how she was working through her anger that week. She would share with me insights she had, different perspectives she discovered, the levels of acceptance she was creating.

At the sixth session, Gertie sat down and shared the following with me. Please understand that what follows is an approximation, but the directness and clarity of it are all Gertie's, and a true representation of her.

"Dr. John, I believe I am okay. Today, I can let my anger go. Here is what has changed for me. These are my new understandings. As hard as it is to say, I see and accept my brother had some responsibility for that tragedy, for he put himself there in harm's way. He didn't deserve to die! But he did have responsibility. And I can accept that.

I understand that my brother was doing the best that he could. He had an illness, and though he had responsibility for managing his illness, and he failed at that, he was still driven by that illness to seek drugs. I can accept this.

I understand that the two young men who killed my brother had both come from very troubled childhoods, and very traumatic circumstances. This doesn't excuse them—what they did was still wrong. It does help me to understand them and what drove them to be at that place and to act in violence. I can accept that they both were acting out of their own hurts and wounds. And I can accept this truth about them.

I understand that I have been trapped in this nightmare, because I thought justice and revenge...actually, what *I* thought was justice, and what *I* believed was righteous revenge...had to be served. The two men *had* to pay the full price *for me to honor my brother, and for me to be okay*. And I realize now, that's not true.

I understand that I've been so focused on trying to *make* the system work *the way I wanted*, that I let myself become focused on what was out of my control. I can't make the justice system do just what I want. I can share my voice and my perspective, but I have to let go of the outcomes, or I'll remain trapped in my anger for the rest of my life.

I understand that I can let my brother go. I am still sad that he is dead. I still wish he were here. But he's not, and I can accept that this tragedy happened. I can accept my brother's death, and that I continue to die by remaining stuck in my anger.

I can forgive those two men. Over the years, as I've listened to them at parole hearings, I have come to believe that one of them is truly remorseful, and truly ashamed for what he did. I believe this man has changed, and I believe he should be allowed to reclaim his life. And because of that… because of the changes he's made, his real expression of sorrow and acceptance of his failure, and the time he has served… because of these things, I won't oppose his parole. In fact, I am willing at this point to speak for his parole. I believe he deserves a second chance at life.

The other man, I don't see any, or many changes in him. He is still resentful, he still blames others and the system for what happened, and he is in complete denial that he did anything wrong. For him, I will still speak against his parole. I will say my piece, and then I believe I can let go of the decision. I can accept whatever the courts decide to do."

Gertie's eyes were clear like I hadn't seen them before. Her face was smoothed and unlined of the distress and anguish she had carried for so many years.

"Dr. John, I am okay. Actually, I'm better than okay. I feel freed. Liberated. It is time for me to live my life, to let the past be in the past, and to set my anger aside. You know, I've even had to forgive myself, for holding onto my anger for so long. I was doing the best I could; I couldn't have let it go sooner. But I can let it go now."

That was my last session with Gertie. I told her how amazed I was at the courage she showed, to shift and expand her understanding, to accept and to forgive. And I told her what a privilege it was to have sat with her as she found her way to healing and health. For in those six sessions, she did all the work; I rarely and barely talked. I just listened, and infrequently offered a different perspective.

I will always remember and remain impressed with Gertie and her self-healing. Remarkably, profoundly impressed. I was so glad for her. And I was grateful too, for Gertie became such a hopeful model to me of what a person can do to save themselves from emotional wounds.

A closing word on hurt, anger's always companion. Hurt is healed by the same schema as anger.

When we are hurt, we will need to identify it, clarify it, give it expression (venting), develop a plan and look forward. We will need to practice the tasks of understanding, acceptance and forgiveness.

We will also need three other things. Comfort. Hope. And realistic optimism. Healing hurt will require us to soothe ourselves, to give ourselves comforts in small yet meaningful ways. We will need to be able to look forward and believe life can be good again. And we will need to see the changes and steps we can take to come back to life and to enjoying life.

Of the Mind

Mindfulness. Most people have heard of it, and learned something about it. In my work, and in my own life, I have found mindfulness to be incredibly helpful, though it is hard sometimes to put into practice. Actually, it is hard to consistently and persistently (the first two of C'PADH) maintain the practice of it. This is because, in my perspective, the basic concepts of mindfulness run so counter to what we have grown up with and inculcated into our mind.

The basic tenets of mindfulness, as I understand them, are.... Well, pretty basic.

The practice of radical acceptance.

Do one thing at a time.

Do what works.

Apply the art of d'BLARD.

There is no judgement. There is no failure.

Let's look at these separately.

The practice of radical acceptance. What the hell does that mean?! What is *radical* acceptance? What is radical about it? And how in the hell can that help me?

Great questions...wish I had the answers.

Hahaha—I funny! I made joke there!

Radical acceptance is the acceptance of everything, as it is. Now, acceptance does not mean approval. We can find something abhorrent, evil, and wrong, and still accept that it exists.

But why do this? There is a very specific reason for this practice; it allows us to give up regrets, to let go of wanting our past to be different, of believing that something else outside of us has to change for us to be okay. In some classic language, radical acceptance helps us move from an *external* locus of control to an *internal* locus of control. It helps us to keep our focus on ourselves and our changes, what we need to change with ourselves, and not get trapped by the changes we want other people to make, or the changes we want in situations.

If the term radical acceptance is unappealing to you, here's a synonym: grace. Being gracious, observing others and ourselves with grace, is exactly the same as radical acceptance. At least it is in my mind.

Do one thing at a time. I chuckle with bemusement when I hear people tell me they are excellent at multi-tasking. I think to myself, 'Does his wife think he's excellent at multi-tasking? Does her husband think she's great at multi-tasking? Do those you work with appreciate, or like, or even believe, that you're a model multi-tasker?' I bet not, because the research I've seen on multi-tasking reports that *no one* truly multi-tasks! Whether that research is accurate or not (and I believe it is for the vast majority of us as humans, and for the vast majority of times), multi-tasking or trying to divides our attention. Such a behavior diffuses our awareness. We lose touch with the moment, and what we are doing *this moment*, which takes away the sense of being fully alive, engaged with and enjoying our life.

This is why the practice of doing one thing at a time is so valuable, because when we struggle with the pains and wounds we have suffered, we are so often taken out of living our life. We get pulled away from being present in this moment, and get trapped in the past or in the future. To truly enjoy and revel in our life, even the most mundane aspects of it like washing the dishes or weeding the garden or brushing our teeth, we need to be present. We need to be here, now, and nowhere else.

Do what works. The goal behind this principle is to help us break out of our patterns, to escape from the traps of "what we should do" and "what is acceptable and what is not," and free ourselves to find what works for us. For you.

It makes me a little crazy when I read or hear of someone who makes the claim "…and this is sure to work for you. Guaranteed." What bullshit. Nothing, *nothing*, works for everyone. One of the biggest challenges I face when working with you as patients is to help you listen to yourselves, to help you discover and decide what works for you, even if it doesn't work for anyone else.

Find what works, for you. Do what works, for you. Live your life, not anyone else's.

Apply the art of d'BLARD. The use of these five skills (deep Breathe, Let Go, Accept, Relax, Detach…just in case you forgot, or skipped over that part), are invaluable when learning to practice mindfulness and live mindfully. These five skills help us to become grounded in the present and to stay present here in this moment of our life.

There is no judgement. There is no failure. This principle is so difficult for us, having grown up in a culture where success and failure are such a dominant part of the fabric and framework of our lives. We have absorbed to the point of absoluteness the notions of "right and wrong," "good and bad," "winner and loser," "better and worse." We can barely question them.

The challenge for us, as we heal our emotional wounds, is to realize that these structures can and most often are harmful to our healing and health. Judgement and criticism are rife with negative self-thoughts, and it is negative beliefs that sustain painful emotions. As we learn to shift our beliefs and perceptions, we can simply *describe* aspects of life, people and ourselves instead of judging them.

A personal note on the power of shifting away from negative, critical judgements and to descriptions. In my work, I often have to share with a person something very difficult to hear. I have to (more accurately, I choose to) share with them very painful observations. Some examples may help.

Example #1. A woman is working on her relationship with her husband, complaining how difficult he is, and shares a conversation with him that she believes indicates how he doesn't listen to her. When he asked her how he could demonstrate love to her, she tells me her response was "If you'd listen to me, you'd know." And I choose to share with her, "Winnie, do you realize your response to your husband was passive-aggressive?"

Example #2. A man tells me about an argument with his wife, where "she pissed me off so bad, I threw my keys on the couch, told her what a fucking bitch she was, and that her lack of wanting sex was the only problem in the marriage." I share with him, "Willard, do you realize that because she was sitting on the couch, she experienced your throwing the keys as aggression *towards her?* And, that name calling is never acceptable and always harmful? And, that she may not want to have sex with you after you've called her names and she feels threatened and you tell her she's *the only problem in the relationship?*"

In both these instances, I was fortunate enough to make my responses mere descriptions and not judgements or criticisms. I was able to do this by the tone of my voice, by the pitch of my voice, and mostly, because I *believed*, I held the belief, that it was not my place to judge, only to share. Thank the stars and word fairies, both people were able to hear my responses and see their own behaviors in a different perspective.

It has been my experience that when we move away from criticism of others and ourselves, and shift to mere observations and descriptions, we open ourselves to much healthier and more satisfying life and relationships.

Try the shift. Listen to yourself, and identify where you are critical and judgmental of yourself, and then try shifting to simply describing and observing. What I find happens is, we begin to discover so much more about ourselves, we uncover answers and explanations and reasons that we couldn't when we were merely criticizing ourself. When we find these new discoveries, we are on the path to changing, healing and health.

Which reminds me of another Stuhlism.

Stuhlism #21

There are always reasons. There are always answers.

This, of course, refers to relationships, our relationship with ourself and our relationship with others. We all know there is no final answer for the number pi, or how many grains of sand there are in the Sahara, or why is there even a reason for Oklahoma. But in relationships, with others and especially with ourselves, there are always reasons. And there are always answers.

Now, the reasons may not be very reasonable; they may not be very logical or realistic. But the reasons for our behaviors and our choices, and for others' choices and behaviors, are there; it just takes effort, a real, concerted effort to find them and bring them to light.

This effort is marked by some specific strategies. The first is, as you work to understand a problem, or hurt or conflict with someone, identify what you already know (or think you know) and then set those knowns aside. We do this because what we already know hasn't solved the confusion or the hurt or the pain. We have to dig into what we *don't* know.

The second strategy is, do *not* settle for "I don't know." "I don't know" is the death of healing and growth.

Refuse to accept it; be curious, be persistent, look for other perspectives and other possibilities.

The third strategy is an essential accompaniment to the second; when we've reached the end of what we know, and haven't achieved an answer or healing, and can't think of something new or see with a new perspective, *then* is the time to start making up some answers to our questions. Be creative, be inventive—at this point any possibility can begin new discovery and can help us find the path to healing. The term "brainstorming" has been around forever, at least since I was a kid (which, I know, for many of you probably means "since forever"); that is what is encouraged here. Brainstorm with yourself, and when you're stuck, make up stuff. Sometimes the wackier and more far-fetched the better, because at least it gets your mind working and whirling and whizzing and fizzing; when that happens, all kinds of gems begin to fall out of our unconscious and into our awareness.

The fourth strategy takes courage and practice, because it is the strategy of listening to our intuition. "How is it practiced, Dr. John?" asks Editor Queen. "How is listening to our intuition practiced?" (OMG, *everything* has to be explained to this woman! Wait—did I just type that out loud? Ignore that, please and thank you.)

One of the best ways I've found to practice listening to my intuition is via journaling. My experience and belief is that journaling is second only to therapy for healing. And this is how I use journaling to hear my intuitions.

I start with whatever is worrying me…sometimes I begin with "What is troubling me?", and I start writing possibilities. I'll use categories: my work, or friendships, or feelings of depression. As I develop answers to my questions of "what am I struggling with?", I listen to my inner self and voice. Remember I mentioned that aspect of resonating with the truth? Well, here is a good place to apply it.

Let's say I'm working to identify what is bothering me. I ask myself, "Am I anxious about something?", but that doesn't feel right in my mind, heart, and gut. I ask, "Am I scared about something?" Again, that doesn't click. I keep asking "What is it?" and "Why is it?" Then I ask, "Am I depressed?" Click! When we hit on what is true within us, we resonate. "Yes! I'm feeling depressed. But what am I depressed about?" I'm not sure, so, *I keep asking. I keep searching. I keep generating possibilities, and as I do, my own unconscious wisdom will lead me to the correct answers.*

One of the keys is to keep at it. Keep asking yourself "what? why? how?". And, as you begin to identify answers within, continue asking "Is that all? Is there more that's

troubling?" I truly believe your inner voice will chat you up—
our inner voice yearns to be heard, to share the wisdom that
our inner self…soul, image of god, spark of life, unconscious,
psyche, the universe within, Eugene, however you name
it…holds.

This exercise of learning to listen to our own intuition
is a beautiful practice, and it is one of the most rewarding
practices in which I engage regularly. Possibly better than the
baking of cookies. But just barely better than the
consumption of cookies.

So often in our lives, we have shut ourselves off from
our own inner wisdom. We've been taught not to listen to
our gut, to hush our inner voice for the louder ones outside
us. I believe this is extremely detrimental to our health,
healing, and well-being. We are greatly helped by our own
selves when we find and claim our own inner wisdom.

I believe that's enough mindfulness for one day,
which is quite the statement in and of itself. Let's move on by
going back to something I skipped over.

A Frightening Experience

Trauma and resultant Post Traumatic Stress Disorder are horrible wounds. And what constitutes a trauma is wide and varied. I've worked with military veterans whose trauma wasn't combat, but rather some of the horrible living conditions they witnessed in the country they were in. I've had one person whose trauma was the death of her husband, a death that was made so much more wounding because the husband wouldn't accept that he was dying, so there was no way for the woman to say good-bye, because we can't say good bye to someone who's "not dying," because he wouldn't let her. And of course, I have had over a hundred patients with traumas arising from sexual abuse, physical abuse, abandonment, emotional abuse, or medical malpractice. What constitutes a trauma is really dependent upon the person's reaction to the initiating event. Trauma is when some experience is so intense that our natural, innate coping mechanisms (our Adaptive Information Processing capacity) are so flooded with sensations that they are unable to process the experience. We are then left with the experience as *an experience*, with all the thoughts and emotions and sensations of the experience, instead of simply a memory.

Why this happens, we do not know. My own hypothesis is that at that certain points in time when a person experiences a trauma and it is not processed, the person's cognitive structures and guiding principles and values are in significant conflict, and the person is confused at an existential level. The presence of a trauma, then, is not an indication of a weakness, a weak mind, but rather, just the opposite; it is the indication of a mind that is confronting the inequities of life and striving to make sense of the presence of evil in the world.

No matter the instigating event, there are several constants across traumas. One is that the person who witnesses or experiences the traumatic event, experiences it as overwhelming. This may not occur immediately; in fact, most of the time, it takes quite some time for the trauma aspect of the experience to emerge and manifest. However long it takes, once the wounds of the trauma begin to come into the person's awareness, then the trauma infiltrates nearly every aspect of their life.

Another constant across all traumas is that the person feels powerless in relation to the symptoms of the trauma wound. Flashbacks, intrusive thoughts and images, nightmares, hypervigilance and hypersensitivity—some or all of these symptoms blast into the person's life, unwittingly and at seemingly random, inappropriate, and unacceptable times. The person suffering the emergent symptoms of trauma feels caught in a maelstrom of the most intense, painful emotions and experiences, and feels completely at the mercy of these symptoms. As those of you who've suffered or still suffer PTSD know, it is a nightmare of existence. And I'm sure I'm not even doing your experience justice in my descriptions; I'm certain that at times I did not heard you thoroughly or reflect accurately the depth, difficulty, pain, and distress you experienced. That was due to my limited ability to fully enter into your experience, and my lack of connection at those moments. For those, I do apologize.

A third constant across all traumas is that while the person feels out of control, they don't lose complete control, and so they remain unbelievably confused. "What the hell is happening to me?" is the most frequent question.

Yet another constant: almost everyone initially feels weak, like a failure, and blames themself. As I said earlier, this is always, always inaccurate—a person who suffers a trauma is a victim of an emotional wound, and is innocent. One of the crucial steps of healing is to realize this, believe it and embed that belief in order to resolve and dismiss the feelings of shame, guilt and embarrassment, of weakness and failure and despair, emotions that do not belong to be associated with the traumatic event and that are such hurdles to healing.

One more constant (at least, the last one I can think of right now): when a person suffering from PTSD hears the diagnosis and begins to understand and believe it, there is an initial experience of relief. This is actually true for all the mental disorders and illnesses; in fact, it is so true, I can make it a Stuhlism.

Stuhlism #22

An accurate diagnosis of a mental disorder or illness is a relief, and acceptance of that diagnosis is a key step in beginning to heal.

"Why, you ask? What's good about knowing you have an identifiable mental illness or disorder, Dr. J?"

Excellent question. I can share with you the answers many of you have shared with me.

"Thank god...there's a reason why this is happening to me."

"You mean, I'm not alone? I'm not the only one who struggles like this?"

"Ohhhh...now it all makes sense!"

"You mean, I'm not crazy?!"

And my response to the last is always, "No, you're not crazy. That's a word I don't use...at least in a professional way; there are crazy people: sky divers, free rock

157

climbers, mimes...or, as my editor pointed out, the truly crazy—a sky-diving mime; but no, you are not crazy. You are suffering from an illness, a disorder, and you are not alone."

Because PTSD is one of the worst of the mental illnesses, arising out of the most intense wounds, I can't begin to cover it all here. What I would want any patient who has suffered PTSD to know is this.

There is hope. There is healing. There is recovery. There really, truly is hope, healing, and recovery...hold on to those three, even if they don't *feel* true.

The fact that the flashbacks and nightmares, the symptoms, are emerging, is actually a good sign. It means that our inner self, our unconscious where our inner wisdom resides, is telling us "We are ready to heal." This too can be a Stuhlism.

Stuhlism #23

Our inner self, our unconscious, has a wisdom with regards to healing. When we become aware of our emotional hurts and wounds, it is our inner wise self-communicating to us that we need healing, *and are ready to begin healing!*

Healing does not necessarily mean a return to the same self we were prior to the trauma. We may heal, and be a much different person. Thus, it is important not to measure our healing/healed self against our prior self. As one patient put it to me…"I used to think that my PTSD wasn't healed until I was just like the person I was before the traumas. But now I know that's not true; I'll always carry some aspect of the trauma, just as I might heal from a leg injury, yet always walk with a limp." Smart patient; wish I'd been that smart as a therapist, to suggest that perspective to him. I couldn't then…but I can share it now, with you.

There is so much more I could write about trauma, but I don't want this to be a textbook. For those of you who are still struggling with your PTSD, I'm sure this isn't enough. I apologize—I wish I had more time and space. If this isn't enough to see you through, let me encourage you to persist in getting help, and to not give up. Because I do also believe that PTSD almost always requires the help of at least one other person, and usually more. It is such a devastating wound that rarely can we heal all on our own. Seek help, accept help and keep pursuing help until you find the healing you desire and deserve.

Tidying Up

I realize I could go on and on. Damn, I didn't realize I had that much to say, or even had that many words in my head. But the goal of this was not to cover absolutely everything I know and think and believe; the goal is for it to maybe, hopefully, possibly be of assistance to you when I am retired and no longer available to you.

Not that you can't find an excellent therapist. I'm hopeful you can and will find one, and that they'll be able to help you even more than I have (I know—big assumption there). But since I have been with many of you for a good length of time, or what may seem like your whole life, I wanted you to have these few thoughts and beliefs.

I realize that what I'm putting in your hands is very simplistic, and that I have glossed over, omitted or not recognized all the complexities that go into the discipline of healing and of living healthy. I'm sorry about the simplicity, and apologize if there are not enough how to's.

Because I'm reaching the endurance of my editor (a god of word counts who severely punishes if I exceed), I thought I'd close with some loosely aligned notions.

On Relationships

In any loving, committed relationship, love is not enough.

The key to longevity and quality in a relationship is not love, or good sex, or   compatibility, or even good communication. The key is hard work.

Almost any two people, who are both willing to work at it, can make a mutually satisfying relationship.

If I want to change a relationship, *I* have to change.

It is reasonable and realistic to ask for reasonable and realistic changes.

If you need to be "right" in a relationship, it means that you need the other to be wrong. The psychological term for this is "… Oh, you're screwed…". Give up right and wrong, and graduate to understanding.

If we are frustrated, disappointed or angry with another, it means that we haven't set our expectations of them low enough.

Detachment is one of the highest, if not the highest, forms of love.

On Emotions, Change, and Choices

Frustration is when we have a goal, and are blocked in getting to it. The first step in resolving frustration is to identify the goal, and ask "Is this goal in my control?" If it is not (as in, it involves a change in another person), then we need to restructure our goal so that it is in our control. Only then will our frustration subside.

Heightened emotions tell us:
1. we are taking things personally, and
2. alert us to where we are uncomfortable with ourselves.

She-who-rules-my-words demands an explanation. So, let's see: when I am completely comfortable with an aspect of myself, then there is nothing external to me that can cause me feelings of distress about it. Therefore, the opposite is also true: when I have feelings of distress (anger, defensiveness, anxiety, fear, embarrassment, shame, etc.) then those feelings tell me *something about me!* They tell me I have some discomfort, not that the discomfort is external to me.

Any change we make, even if the change we make is expressly for another, is still a change we make for ourselves. OMG! This woman struggles with every damn thought! I mean, damn it's helpful for her to point out where I need more elucidation. Let me give an example: I look up from my life one day and realize, "Holy cow flops, John; you have been a stingy, miserly bastard, haven't you?" And so, wanting to develop a soul, even in these latter years, I think "I'm giving 90% of my money away this year!" My goal is to practice charity, generosity and to help others by sharing what I have. And this action *still* is a change I make for myself. For, you see, in my recognition of my mingy, uncharitable ways, I felt a need to make a change. *I* needed to change; *I* needed to feel charitable. I made that change, from scrimpy to unstinting, for *my* need. Maybe the next thought will help.

Every choice we make, every action we choose, in fundamentally selfish: it serves us in some way.

When we practice sufficiency, we need to pause and evoke the feelings of calm and settled-ness, of being grounded, of quietude and peace. The *experience* of these feelings sustains and enhances healthy living.

One of the great skills in life is to discover and know our wishes, our hopes, our expectations, and embrace them *without needing them*.

I don't need anything external to me to change for me to be okay.

On Language and Communication

The most effective, influential language in most instances is C'PADH language: Consistent, Persistent, Assertive, Direct, and Honest.

When we offer a compliment, take the time to make sure the compliment is received. If it is deflected or ignored, share with the other, "You know I was complimenting you, right? I really did mean that compliment."

When given a compliment, take a moment and acknowledge it. A simple, "Thank you!" will usually suffice.

"No" is a complete sentence. Additions to "no" are multiple opportunities for the other to overturn our "no."

"Yes" is a complete sentence. Living by affirmations makes life so much more enjoyable.

"Because" is never, *ever* an acceptable answer!

Try to eliminate qualifiers and expand enhancers.
"I think I'm a good person"
becomes
"I am a good person."
And,
"You are thoughtful"
becomes
"You are really a very thoughtful person."

Try to eliminate ambiguity.
"Maybe I'd like to try snow skiing"
becomes
"I'd like to try snow skiing."
Actually, I'd trade my children to live on the side of a ski slope, and ski every day for six months. Snow skiing may be better than life—I hope the afterlife is one long, lovely ski trip. But I digress.

On Honoring Ourselves and the Present Moment

We have all we need within ourselves.
Self-love is sufficient.
Self-worth is sufficient.
Self-esteem is sufficient.
Self-acceptance is sufficient.
Self-approval is sufficient.
Self-security is sufficient.
Self-care is sufficient.
Self-validation is sufficient.

Any emotional need we have, we have the power ourselves to satisfy.

Critical, judgmental, negative self-talk leads to anxiety.

There is only today. Make today good.

Our greatest emotional and personality strength is also our greatest weakness. Apparently, my editor has developed EDD (Explanation Deficiency Disorder). So, here's an example of this tidbit. Say one of my greatest strengths is being considerate (I'm not saying this is true; my greatest strength is probably napping). I am thoughtful of others, I look for ways to be of help to others, I want to put others' needs before mine. What then occurs in my relationships is that I get taken advantage of much more easily that others; I end up paying little attention to my own needs and wants; I struggle to hear myself because I'm so busy listening to others. This is what I mean by our greatest strength is also our greatest weakness.

For you to have what you want and what you need, others are going to have to pay a price, and that's okay.

I realized, decades ago, that I had enough interests for about three lifetimes. For me to enjoy this lifetime, I had to focus on the choices I was making, all I was saying "yes" to, and let go of all the things I said "no" to. Otherwise, all my days would be filled with frustrations.

Every choice has benefits and costs, positives and negatives, advantages and disadvantages. The trick is to find the ones you don't already know.

When I say "yes" to one thing in my life, I say "no" to a whole bunch of other things. And this is okay! We can't say yes to everything.

This one is hard, especially in our religious culture: There are no saviors. Everyone has to become their own savior. Throughout our life, others may help; people may be an incredible gift to us, but ultimately, every person has to save himself or herself.

On Healing

For us to resolve a hurt or wound, or clarify a confusion, we don't need anyone else's participation. We don't need the other person to "understand," we don't need the other person to "see," we don't need the person to "agree," or "recognize," or "get it." We don't need anything from the other person for us to resolve what is within us.

Our minds crave information; life is more enjoyable when we learn how to feed our mind.

Our minds want to show us what we need to heal, and how to heal.

Emotional and psychological healing generalizes, and emotional health spreads.

Exercise is medicine. In fact, it is the most under-utilized medicine we have. Regular, moderate exertion improves the performance and satisfaction of every organ and structure of our body and mind.

Our bodies crave exertion just like our lungs crave oxygen. Our bodies also crave comfort. We have become obsessed with the latter, and lost touch with the former.

The four areas where we can most easily improve our quality of life is with exercise, nutrition, sleep, and structure or order.

As we heal, we will discover inequities and injustices that we have suffered. A healing step is to ask ourselves the question "Since this is the unfairness I've experienced, can I accept that and live well in spite of it?" Hopefully the answer will always be yes.

Psychological, emotional wounds are harder to heal than physical ones. Therefore, they require more intentional effort. My editor-of-my-life questions the significance of this maxim and suggests this tidbit of wisdom might be trimmed; my response to her is that's fine with me, if she really felt it added little. I mean, it's wounding because it was my first insight, back when I was 4, but okay, fine. Just take it out. It won't bother me. I'll get over the pain. I always do. And then I added, but what do you think about letting my patients decide if it's helpful to them. I guess Ms. Word Guru decided to let you decide. Good decision, I think.

For our finest living, we embrace our illness.

Most healing is hard. When we begin to heal, ask ourselves, "Can I do hard things?" Then answer, "Yes."

In healing, we have to find what we *don't* know. We have to discover the emotions that we are experiencing but are unaware of.

One of the crucial elements in healing is to give yourself successes. The smaller the success, the better (that whole "single iota" idea). And we need to stay with the success long enough that we can *feel* the success, not simply know it.

Nothing…no skill, no strategy, no exercise, no practice, no discipline… nothing works all the time. We need a vast array of resources in our healing tool chest.

One of the two places where the bible got it right is…the truth, our truth, always sets us free.

It takes more strength to admit our hurts and emotional wounds than it takes to deny them. It takes less effort to heal than it does to deny our need for healing. That is why healing always frees us.

Become a magnet for health, an intense gravitational pull for wellbeing, by healing well yourself.

As we make our way on the path of healing, we will find we have many questions. Any time, and every time, we ask ourselves a question, we need to generate an answer or answers. Unanswered questions leave us with more anxiety; answers tend to settle us.

Medications don't "fix" the person, they don't "make the person focus," or "make the person see reality," or stop the depression/anxiety/grief/confusion. Medications treat the illness and disability within the person; it is you, the individual, who then makes life good. Medication removes the obstacles, so that *your true self comes through.*

This last one seems in direct contradiction to my earlier statistic. Remember when I said (what seems like eons ago), that 98.7% of the time, it has nothing to do with you? Well, that Stuhlism is still true. Its accompanying belief is: When healing, no matter what has happened to us, the healing and changes *always come back to me!* In a real sense, it doesn't matter what happens *to* us, it is what we *do* with what happens to us. Thus...

Our healing, our recovery, our good life, is all about us. Our healing is all in our own hands, because ultimately, it is all about you. It is all up to you.

So, Our Session Is About to Conclude

It is time to close, which makes me sad, because I am going to miss you. And, I am going to miss this writing. I'll leave you with a couple final ideas that guide me.

The first is...

I have come to believe that if a person can give an unequivocal "Yes" to the following three questions, then life is pretty good.

1. Am I glad to be alive?

2. Am I glad to be me?

3. Am I glad for my life, the life I've lived?

And the second is...

There are two poles that I try to live between.

1. You are of ultimate worth, and value, and beauty, just the way you are. You don't have to change one damn thing to be good enough. You are good enough right now, just as you are.

2. I am of no more value or worth or beauty, and deserve nothing more, than any other person on this planet.

If I can live between these poles, I can be glad for my worth and value and beauty. I can revel in this life I have, and be proud of who I am and who I've tried to make myself. And, I can remain humble and grateful for this life which I did nothing to deserve, and feel infinite gratitude for this life that comes to me as a privilege alone.

Thank you, for the years of trust. Thank you for the privilege and pleasure of working with you. Thank you, for the honor of sharing your lives with me. And if you've made it this far, thank you for your endurance and patience.

I go now to write a second novel.

I go alone.

But Wait…There's One Last Thing

Why do I think of you as friends? Why do I see my patients in the framework of friendship? I believe I promised you above I'd explain. Here's why.

There are several modalities I use in therapy. One, I use a cognitive behavioral approach, to look at cognitions and behaviors and how we can adjust them. Second, I use an existential approach to therapy, as I believe there are certain existential dilemmas we all face in life, and to identify, confront and resolve them leads to much more healthy, rich living. Third, I use affective therapy, to focus on feelings and emotions, and how to embrace them and free ourselves in life with them. Fourth, I use psychodynamic therapy, because what we've experienced in the past I believe greatly shapes and affects us. Fifth, most importantly, and the reason for this addendum, is that I have always practiced interpersonal therapy.

What does that mean? It means that I have always tried to have a real relationship with you, with any patient. With every patient. I have always tried to be genuine and authentic; I have always tried to be open, honest and self-disclosing. I have shared with you my thoughts and perspectives, I've intentionally allowed you to know what you

172

wanted about my life and living so that you'd know I was a real person with real struggles, hurts, joys, successes, distresses, and fuck ups, just like everyone else. I've offered hypotheses as we sought to find healing and understanding. And maybe most importantly, I've been more than willing to be wrong in my perceptions and hypotheses.

To practice therapy this way means sharing a closeness with another, with you. And I can't be that close with just a "patient." It takes a friendship, a mutual relationship of support and trust and love and disclosure, and I never thought I could develop that kind of healing relationship without a true friendship. I chose to provide therapy this way because I believed it was the best path of healing for you, for patients.

Of course, the relationship wasn't equal; after all, I got paid, and you didn't. And I was there to provide help for you, but not there for you to provide healing for me (that's why I have my journal). But my goal was to help you feel a closeness that was real and genuine, and care that was safe and supportive and most helpful. My hope was that I helped to make the relationship equitable, so that you felt you got more than you hoped for, found more help than anticipated and found healing you thought impossible.

I'm confident that I didn't always succeed; and for the times I wasn't helpful or supportive enough or wise enough, I do apologize. My hope was that you consistently and persistently felt safe, cared for, loved, cherished, and believed in; that you found help and healing via our sessions, and that the relationship itself was a means of healing by allowing you to relate to another person with the certain safety that you could say anything, share anything and explore anything, knowing and experiencing that you were never judged or criticized, condemned or disdained.

My belief, my hope, and my experience is that through such a relationship, we come to know and accept ourselves, just as we are, because who we are has been reflected to us by another.

Lofty goals, I know. Idealistic, possibly. I hope that I came close, and that you found comfort and restoration in our time together, not just in the therapy I provided, but also in the relationship we created together. If that occurred, I am immeasurably glad.

With that, I do truly close, and go to write my second novel.

And I still go alone.

A Thanks

You haven't really met her, but you've heard about her. You've eaves-dropped on my inner chatting with her (kinda rude, but you're forgiven). You've seen her influence on me, in the best of ways, because without her, this long, chaptered letter would truly be a word jumble. You may even have developed some mental constructs and images of her—all of them will be woefully inadequate and insufficient to the wonder that is her real self.

So, join me please, in saying a most heartfelt and grateful thank you to Ms. Rebecca Warren, editor, Goddess of Grammar, Empress of my wandering Imaginings, and such a dear, good friend. She has been indispensable to me in the creation of this little work, and believe me, a real blessing to you, if you've read this far.

Thank you, Rebecca.